DISCOVERY, CREATIVITY AND PROBLEM-SOLVING

For

Kerry Lamb and Craig Lamb

Discovery, Creativity and Problem-Solving

DAVID LAMB

Department of Philosophy
University of Manchester

Avebury

Aldershot · Brookfield USA · Hong Kong · Singapore · Sydney

© D. Lamb 1991

Published by

Avebury
Academic Publishing Group
Gower House
Croft Road
Aldershot
Hants GU11 3HR
England

Gower Publishing Company
Old Post Road
Brookfield
Vermont 05036
USA

A CIP catalogue record for this book
is available from the British Library.

ISBN 1-85628-043-8

Printed in Great Britain by
Billing & Sons Ltd, Worcester

Contents

I would like to express my thanks to Tracy Russell for the final preparation of the manuscript.

Introduction

The thesis that the process of scientific and artistic discovery is amenable to rational analysis - as opposed to irrational leaps of genius - has not been popular this century. This is due to two factors: a romantic heroic belief in creative genius, and the influence of logical empiricism in the early twentieth-century, which ruled that a logic of the sciences is exclusively a logic of justification. Consequently, for many philosophers scientific discovery was held to be of interest only to historians, psychologists and sociologists, but was barred from the list of topics which demand logical analysis by philosophers.

Against this view it will be argued here that the processes of creativity and discovery are fit subjects for philosophical inquiry; that a rational account of creative discovery processes is possible, and that such an account reveals i) that there is no qualitative distinction between the context of discovery and the context of justification; ii) that for the purpose of philosophical analysis there is no qualitative distinction between discoveries associated with normal and revolutionary periods in science.

As a rule philosophers of science have been concerned with normative rather than descriptive aspects of scientific methodology. In this respect Wittgenstein's injunction to describe rather than prescribe has fell on deaf ears. With few exceptions philosophers of science have been more concerned with how scientists ought to proceed, in conformity with certain conceptions of logic, than with how they do proceed. Ideas concerning how scientists ought to proceed have been traditionally based on theories of truth-maximisation, methodologies designed as protection from skepticism, and have been concerned with the problem of induction, on how generalisations can be validly derived from data on particulars, and on the extent to which data can confirm a generalisation. These are, no doubt, interesting philosophical questions in their own right, but they bear marginal relation to the practice of scientists who frequently encounter philosophical problems of an entirely different kind. Because of their extreme generality, formulations of Cartesian or Humean skepticism, and methodological strategies designed as safeguards against them, play no part in the selection of scientific problems and solution strategies. For this reason Cartesian and Humean based methodologies have little to offer practical scientists.Now it may be desirable if philos -ophers pursue different philosophical problems to those pursued by scientists. It may even be acceptable to refer to their activities as 'philosophy of science'. No interests are harmed. But those who pursue them should not attribute to these reflections any normative significance, or derive from them principles according to which certain aspects of scientific practice are deemed 'irrational', and beyond the scope of philosophical investigation.

Arguments supporting the two-context theory and the belief that discovery is not amenable to rational analysis will be examined in Chapter I. Chapter II focuses on irrationalist explanations of discovery processes and creative thinking, calling into question the age old distinction between art and science, according to which the former is characterised by inexplicable insights whilst the latter possesses a rational component. The account of irrationalist models of discovery in Chapter II will focus primarily on exponents of the two-context theory, such as Hans Reichenbach and Sir Karl Popper. But it will also be argued that some of their post-positivist critics, such as Michael Polanyi, Paul K. Feyerabend and Arthur Koestler, ultimately fall back on irrationalist explanations of hypothesis generation. The term 'irrationalism' here refers in its strong sense to that which cannot be explained; in its weaker sense it refers to beliefs concerning the limits of possible explanations. Conversely, the term 'rationalism' simply refers to beliefs that discovery processes are amenable to rational explanation and assessment.

The expression 'logic of discovery' refers to rational processes which occur in all aspects of scientific development. But a logic of discovery, it must be stressed, cannot deliver a set of rules for the derivation of theories conclusively from observation, and objections based on the impossibility of devising a fool-proof discovery machine miss the point at issue entirely. It is clearly futile to seek a single scientific method which will explain how hypotheses are generated in activities as diverse as chemistry, physics, astronomy, geology, economics, and psychology. But it is equally futile, although not so readily admitted, to seek a single method for the assessment of already formulated hypotheses in these disciplines.

Undoubtedly many methods can be employed for both drawing hypotheses and assessing them. But the point behind claims on behalf of a logic of discovery is that these methods can be identified, studied, assessed, and possibly improved. Scientists with superior heuristics and better problem solving techniques are more likely to make significant discoveries and take advantage of lucky breaks. The assessment and criticism of techniques employed to enhance (as opposed to guarantee) one's chance of making a discovery is a task which has unfortunately been neglected by philosophers. Such a task would involve nothing more than the search for, and assessment of, criteria for judging the efficiency of processes employed to solve problems. A minimum requirement of a logic of discovery would involve a concept of rationality which endorsed methods for reducing the search for solutions in any problem field.

Rationalist accounts of discovery are introduced in Chapter III which focuses on various attempts to formulate a 'logic of discovery'. This involves an examination of Charles Sanders Peirce and Norwood R. Hanson's retroductive or abductive models of discovery and an assessment of criticism made of this endeavour by P. Achinstein and others. The expression 'logic of discovery' will again refer to the means by which the processes of discovery and creativity can be given a rational explanation. As such to assert that a logic of discovery is possible is to rebut the belief that creative work is is the product of inexplicable forces. References to a logic of discovery are not to 'logic' in any restricted sense, by which is meant the procedures of formal logic, but simply to accounts of the reasoning processes which feature in problem solving tasks. Other models of rationality, which may be linked to particular methodologies, such as verificationism or falsificationism, are left untouched here. When speaking of rationality in relation to discovery making processes, it must be stressed that 'rationality' has never referred to an ability to arrive at the right answer on every occasion. A rational account of the processes involved in discovery will simply outline the reasons bound up with procedures which increase opportunities to solve problems and take advantage of theoretical and experimental developments.

Chapter IV outlines the preconditions for a logic of discovery, rejecting the emphasis frequently placed on 'great moments' in the discovery process, offering as an alternative the suggestion that discovery and creative thinking in general can be seen as a mode of problem solving. It is also argued that the rational element in the discovery process is to be found in the interplay between solution generators and solution restrictors. Chapter V continues this approach with further elaboration of the interplay between procedures employed in both the generation and evaluation of solutions and draws important analogies between problem solving techniques in the sciences, including recent developments in Artificial Intelligence and medical diagnosis. With reference to particular discoveries in the history of science it is argued in Chapter VI that the two-context theory (with its related concepts of discovery and justification as separate events) should be replaced by a concept of discovery as a process with various stages, each one of which is amenable to criticism and assessment. This readmission of discovery is not merely an attempt to extend the scope of methodological assessment; it is an acknowledgement of what the philosophy of science is really about, and is therefore an affirmation of the belief that the status of discovery should be given a prominent position in the same way that the status of justification achieved prominence in the nineteenth century. It must also be stressed that the number of significant stages in the process of discovery which are outlined in Chapter VI are merely a matter of convenience. It is not intended that the two-context theory should be replaced by a three context or a four or five-context theory. What is being proposed is that the entire process of discovery is amenable to rational assessment and possible simulation, and that whilst there are recognisable stages they need not be delineated by rigidly defined boundaries.

Finally, it must be acknowledged that any attempt to characterise the rationality of discovery must run up against powerful metaphysical beliefs attached to the notions of creativity and discovery. These beliefs are bound up with the awe and mystery which thinking people have experienced in their dealings with the world around them. There is an understandable resistance to theories which claim to explain away wonderful and awe-inspiring phenomena, and this resistance frequently protects romantic beliefs that creativity is ultimately irrational. It will be argued here that whilst one of the great tasks of science is to show that awesome and wonderful phenomena are amenable to rational analysis, this is not an attempt to do away with awe and wonder, and replace brilliance with dull mechanistic routine. Rather, it is to recognise that brilliance has been wrongly contrasted with rationality, and that something awesome and wonderful, like the generation and evaluation of a brilliant hypothesis, is not explained away by rational models which break the discovery process down into simple problem solving methods. Instead, it will be maintained that the appreciation of brilliance is actually enhanced by means of an examination of the discovery process, and that this approach can itself

4

generate more wonder - if only over how such simplicity was concealed by complexity.

I Creativity and discovery

Myths About Creativity

From time to time there is a desire among politicians to encourage creativity. The production of new ideas - usually in the sciences - is seen as one of the ways of enhancing national prosperity and well-being. These attempts often begin by posing the following question: 'How can we discover creative potential in our children and youth?' This question is then followed by requests for schemes by means of which 'creative personalities' can be identified and despatched to appropriate institutions which will promote their growth and development. Lurking behind these strategies is often an 'heroic' or 'great man' theory of scientific and cultural development, whereby the pivotal moments of science and culture can be attributed to the heroic efforts of outstanding figures. According to the heroic theory the essential features of the creative process are located within something described as a 'creative personality'. The key to the advancement of knowledge on these terms would be an understanding of the mechanisms by means of which creative personalities can be generated and motivated.

This whole account is both crude and ultimately counter- productive. It ignores the complex variables which contribute to the generation and eventual adoption of novel ideas; it ignores the collective and evolutionary development of scientific knowledge, and above all it ignores the fact that reliance upon so called creative personalities may just as equally impede as it can enhance creative productivity. Almost every step in creative research has been taken in the face of the inhibiting effect of earlier generations of creative individuals. There are as many tales of advances made by those who broke free from the restrictive ideas of Aristotle, Galen and Ptolemy, as there are concerning those attributable to their original greatness.

Heroic theories of creativity are deeply held in the popular image of scientific and artistic research. It is also part of the popular image that the mechanisms by means of which creative personalities generate their novel ideas are inexplicable. For it is widely held that the kernel of creative thinking is steeped in mystery and irrationality. Newton's apple, Watt's kettle, Wallace's delirium in the jungles of the Malay Archepalago from which he allegedly discovered the idea of speciation; Einstein's recollection that General Relativity became vivid to him as a result of a youthful dream in which he tried to follow a beam of light, and Gray's invention of the telephone inspired by the sight of two lads playing with a pair of cans and a piece of string, all reflect the belief that creative works are bizarre achievements accomplished by eccentric personalities in mysterious circumstances. Such myths are further reinforced by literary images of mad scientists creating diabolical products, such as Doctors Frankenstein, Jekyll and Strangelove.

Closely linked to the heroic myths about creativity are two philosophical traditions which stress that nothing informative can be said about creativity. The first tradition goes back to Plato, who held that there was nothing new under the sun; the second one is the romantic tradition which stresses the mysterious and inexplicable nature of the generation of ideas.

According to Plato there was no such thing as having a new concept or a new idea. What appeared as a new idea was merely the recognition of an old one or the new application of a concept. The 'newness' of an idea, on these terms, would be the experience of novelty felt by the person who was fortunate enough to receive it. This can be described with reference to a child who first grasps a mathematical proof, or a concept like the concept of infinity. Or it might be illustrated with reference to the new application of a concept. If Jones says, for example, 'I have only recently discovered that Smith is an alcoholic', the concepts of 'Smith' and 'alcoholic' will remain the same as they were before the discovery: what has changed is the way in which these concepts have been employed.

There is, of course, something absurd in the proposal that new concepts cannot be manufactured. The idea of a 'cold war', for example, was not simply a combination of our concepts of 'cold' and 'war'. The expression 'cold war' referred to a situation whereby a state of war was maintained without actual warfare. The juxtaposition of these concepts was deliberately paradoxical. The old familiar expressions were merely the vehicles for an entirely new concept.

Donald Schon (1969) cites three new concepts which cannot be classified as either products of recollection in Plato's sense or as a new application of old concepts. These include Newton's theory of light; Ralph Ellison's idea of blacks as invisible men, and the idea of a new mechanical fastener.

Romantic myths about the mystery of creativity have survived long into the twentieth century. They appear in scientific biographies, text books on science and verbal anecdotes. They are embedded in the philosophy of science which maintains that the processes by means of which new ideas are generated defy rational analysis and simulation. According to Herbert Simon (1977,p.226):

> The subject of scientific discovery (and creativity generally) has always been surrounded by dense mists of romanticism and downright know nothingism. Even well-informed persons, who do not believe the stork brings new babies, and are prepared to accept an empirical account of biological creation, sometimes baulk at natural explanations of the creation of new ideas. It appears that the human mind is the last citadel of vitalism.

The Creative Process

Explanations of the creative process have been slow to emerge from the period of logical positivism during the first half of the twentieth century when it was neglected and misunderstood. This is partly because discussions about the creative process tend to get immersed - at the very outset - with problems regarding the quality of creative work. To avoid this problem, the quality of creative work will not be discussed here, and it will be assumed that by its very nature creative work has a value. The term 'creativity' will simply refer to the production of relevant new problems and solutions, inventions and innovations, in any field of human endeavour.

The concept of creativity has its origins in the medieval notion of a God who created a universe *ex nihilo*. During the Middle Ages human beings were not seen as creators, and as late as the Renaissance human artists were not deemed to be creators but were imitators or replicators of forms found in nature. This was compatible with traditional epistemologies from Plato to relatively recent times according to which God was the creator and man the contemplator.

In the nineteenth and twentieth centuries the concepts of 'creativity' and the 'creative process' seem to parallel the concepts of the 'natural' and 'natural processes' - if only in their capacity to inspire nonsense ans mystification. In both the arts and the sciences terms like 'creation' and 'discovery' have been bound up with philosophical assumptions concerning nature and reality. Verbs like 'finding' and 'discovering' suggest that nature precedes human activities, and that discovery is the uncovering of what is part of the real world but hidden for some time, and that the facts 'out there' are natural creations that humans strive to capture. Such a metaphysics supports the view that the scientist or artist is a privileged witness to nature. In contrast, terms like 'creativity', 'invention' and 'design', suggest that the facts are artifacts; that scientists and artists impose constructions on nature rather than merely represent it. Taken too literally distinctions between creation and discovery, social and natural phenomena, are unhelpful. For just as the concept of what is natural is mediated by social reality, so conceptions of what are discoverable are mediated by what has been created or invented. The discovery of distant galaxies is largely dependent upon the invention of suitable observational equipment, and so is the natural curiosity to observe them.

Nature and society, discovery and invention, are inseparably linked. Changes in the concept of nature frequently accompany changes in the concepts of creativity and inventiveness. The nineteenth century romantic concept of the natural world led to the idea of travel as a source of scientific and artistic inspiration. Thus at the height of European colonialisation artists like Gauguin and writers such as Conrad as well as scientists such as Darwin and Wallace, travelled to the colonies in search of inspiration.

An analysis of creativity should take into consideration four interrelated factors: 1) physical reality, 2) mental reality (an individual's knowledge or the collective knowledge of a school), 3) social stratification, and 4) culture. Physical reality and mental reality influence what can be discovered and created; culture is primarily influential in determining how it is to be received, and may have a bearing upon what is considered worth discovering or inventing, whilst the social structure influences the creative product in the sense that many important discoveries and inventions are reproductions of the system of social stratification. A scientist has a knowledge of what is physically possible, an idea of what is theoretically acceptable within the community of scientists, and the choice of research topic will be influenced by cultural fashions that may reflect the system of social stratification. Thus, for example, research on heart disease or AIDS reflects not only the physical and theoretical possibilities but also a cultural

9

interest in the subject together with pressure from social groups who feel threatened by these diseases.

The eventual adoption of a theory may also be influenced by a combination of physical, theoretical and cultural factors. Many major seventeenth-century discoveries took place against a background of religious turmoil which cannot be wholly separated from the science of its day. The emergence of scientific medicine is a good example: new medical theories in the seventeenth century were not adopted because of their instantly recognisable empirical truth but were often adopted because they harmonised with theological beliefs. The success of Harvey's theory of the circulation of blood was largely due to his persuasiveness and the empirical evidence from his vivisections, but its adoption was enhanced through its 'compatibility with the dominating influences in people's minds', especially among those with theological objections to the Cartesian account of heartbeat and circulation, who found in Harvey's work 'a system of thought independent of the clashes of religious sects'.(French,1989, pp. 85-6)

To understand the creative process one must always bear in mind the relationship between the creative producer and the above- mentioned background factors. This is not to deny that they are analytically distinct, or to assert that one of these factors necessarily determines the others in some crude mechanistic manner. But in the absence of any understanding of the expectations appropriate to the level of mental reality, culture and stratification, we cannot begin to understand the nature of what is created or discovered or the process out of which the product emerged. Many accounts of creativity focus exclusively on the biographical details of the particular artist or scientist. But insofar as the creator's biography is relevant to an understanding of the product, its relevance must be in terms of its interaction with the wider community. Creative thought is not reducible to psychological processes within individual heads. As Gonzalo Munevar (1989) argues, scientific thinking emerges when beings have evolved rational and collective procedures for recognising and solving problems. The precondition for scientific invention and creativity is the existence of an objective rationality.

The collective and objective nature of science is frequently ignored when scientists speak of creative discoveries. Parallels are drawn between the alleged subjective and irrationalist aspects of artistic creativity and the generation of original scientific hypotheses. Appeals to artistic imagination are an integral feature of the advice given to aspiring scientists. Max Planck (1949,p.109) once said: 'The pioneer scientist must have a vivid intuitive imagination for new ideas, ideas not generated by deduction, but by *artistically* creative imagination'. These remarks, however, are not really about scientific methodology; they are part of the stock of enthusiasm breeding cliches that we have come to expect from outstanding figures. Great scientists are obliged to say inspiring things about their work. These accounts conform with the rules and conventions of autobiographies and after-dinner speeches. Appeals to artistic imagination, to thinking the unthinkable, acting out hunches, dreams and so on, are all good copy, but they do not provide a true record. But then no one wants to read an autobiography or sit through a lecture which stresses nothing more than adherence to dull routine.

When scientists appeal to artistic creativity they frequently rely on irrationalist and subjectivist conceptions of artistic work, whereby new products seemingly emerge from the imagination without any of the constraints imposed by accumulated wisdom and canonical knowledge. The arts of course are notoriously susceptible to romantic myths and tales of instant illumination have been attached to almost every artistic work of any merit - so much that the alleged irrational nature of artistic creativity is virtually its defining characteristic. This mythology has long provided a cornerstone of British education. For many educationalists the mere suggestion of any similarity between art and science would be preposterous. Yet attempts to provide support for the science-arts distinction invariably fall back on half-baked assumptions about the objectivity of science and the subjectivity of the arts; cold facts on the one hand and hot emotions on the other. Nevertheless, the same techniques employed by Merton, Kuhn, De Solla Price, and Feyerabend, to demystify scientific undertakings can be applied to the understanding of artistic creativeness. The similarities between the two enterprises probably outweigh the differences. Few would seriously dispute that the great achievements of art and science have more in common with each other than with mediocre contemporaneous work. But it is not merely the fact that talented minds constitute a group which is distinguished from others irrespective of disciplinary background. The point is that there is greater diversity within the respective sub-fields of the arts and the sciences than between the two domains. The differences between the performing and the visual arts or between astro- physics and mortuary science are probably as great as any difference between art and science.

The experimental method can hardly be cited as an exclusive feature of science. Early drafts of poetry, painter's sketches, early attempts at plays or novels, have all been described in experimental terms. The first night of a play or a movie can be as decisive as any major scientific experiment. Constable, as is well known, maintained that 'painting is a science of which canvasses are an experiment'. Remi Clignet's (1985) study of creativeness in artistic revolutions reveals how they can be understood in Kuhnian and Mertonian terms and how it makes sense to speak of artistic paradigms which are bound up with particular schools or traditions. To have been part of the French 'New Wave' in the 1950's was to share in a set of values and institutional arrangements among film-makers which yielded easier access to producers and distributors. Artists working within a paradigm, no less than scientists, restrict access to work to members of professional societies, academies, guilds, unions and universities. As in the sciences, those artists committed to certain paradigms may close ranks to protect themselves against rivals or dominant orthodoxies. Thus Impressionist painters like Manet, Monet, and Renoir, closed ranks to protect themselves from ridicule, and limited their exhibitions to those who were sympathetic to the movement. There are also exemplars and paradigm setters in the arts, no less than the sciences. Ezra Pound, T.S.Eliot, and Jean Paul Sartre, are all famous not merely for their literary work but for their theoretical statements as to what literature should be.(Clignet,1985,p.66)

Revolutions in the arts also manifest similar qualities to revolutions in the sciences in the fact that they are determined retrospectively and are rarely reversible. This is not to say that earlier work is never revisited but that the return to the past involves reconstitutions mediated by present interests. There is, however, a belief that science exhibits cumulative progress whilst the arts are transcendental although punctuated with spontaneous outbursts of creativity. This belief is groundless. There is both rupture and continuity in the arts and the sciences. What frequently happens is that later events in science often render invisible the very factors which were suggestive of a rupture with the past. At other times scientists and historians actually minimise or exaggerate differences in order to convey an impression of greater or less continuity, as the occasion demands. Whether or not a set of ideas is continuous or discontinuous is very much a matter of convention; in both the arts and the sciences the co-existence of many different paradigms allows historians enough scope to either emphasise or minimise departures from the status quo.

The kinds of prejudice which erects barriers between the methodologies of the arts and the sciences also generates misunderstanding about the creative process in these disciplines. F.E. Sparshott (1981) has shown how unrealistic perceptions of the creative process are ultimately responsible for the assumption that an unambiguous answer can be given to the question 'Where do new ideas come from?' To a scientist or artist working within a tradition with a commonly recognised set of problems, such a question is meaningless. But to the lay-person, looking in from the outside, and probably ignorant of the problems, potential solutions already considered and rejected, maybe equally unaware of the painful - even plodding - steps towards the solution, the completed work may appear like a bolt from the blue. When the expert describes the final and minute step as a piece of inspiration, the lay-person on the outside may see this as an explanation of the entire process. Sparshott (1981,p.52) points out that:

> The layman who asks the writer how he gets his ideas seems to think that such ideas would be forcing themselves spontaneously on a mind as idle as his own. But nothing is more evident to the artist than that he is working on his art, and the layman is not.

A similar confusion between productivity and instant illumination was described by the nineteenth-century philosopher, G.W.F. Hegel, (1975, p.356) who was patently scornful of romantic theories of creativity.

> Those who are called *geniuses* have acquired a particular skill by means of which they make the universal creations of a people into their own work, as others do with other things. What they produce is not their own invention, but the invention of the *entire* nation, or rather the *discovery*, that the nation has discovered its true essence. What really belongs to the artist as such is his formal activity, his particular skill in this mode of representation, and in this he was educated as part of the universal attainment of skill. He is like the man who finds himself among workers who are building a stone arch whose general structure is invisibly present as an idea. He so happens to be last in line: when he puts his stone into place the arch supports itself. As he places his stone he sees that the whole edifice is an arch, says so, and passes for the inventor.

What productive artists and scientists have in common is not a mysterious connection to unknown springs of insight, still less is it access to secret mental processes. It is nothing more than a steady application to their respective branches of art and science. The creative process - whatever it is - is not to be conceived as something over and above the actual production of work which is deemed to be creative. For this reason there is something suspicious about the search for a creative process. Sparshott's (1981, pp.62-3) remarks about the creative process in the writing of poetry are highly relevant to all aspects of innovative work.

> To ask a poet to describe the creative process is to ask him to formulate a rule, or something that will do in place of a

rule, by following which any idle ninny could make a poem. But writing poems is something idle ninnies cannot do without forfeiting their idleness and ninnyhood. A poet is not an idle ninny who just happens to own a sort of magical sausage-machine that he might lend (or of which he might deliver the patent) to his neighbour, like lending a power-mower. If there is a creative process it cannot be a substitute for intelligent work. It must be the way the work is done.

These remarks, however, should not be taken to imply that nothing of value can be said about the creative process. Sparshott has indicated that an essential component of any explanation of creativity must include reference to the motivation and industriousness of the creative worker. That there is no such thing, or mechanism, which corresponds to popular notions of the creative process we can take for granted. But this need not mean that poets and scientists are incapable of explaining the steps by which they arrived at their creations. The poet, Stephen Spender (1970), gave a detailed explanation of the process out of which emerged the following poetic phrase:

A language of flesh and roses.

This may, or may not be, a particularly meritorious piece of poetry, but an assesssment of the quality of the work is irrelevent here; what matters is the manner in which the phrase was generated. Apparently Spender conceived it during a train journey through the Black Country. Looking at a landscape of pitheads and slagheaps, he heard a stranger say, 'Everything here is man made'. This thought coincided with Spender's own reflections on the scene and was the moment when the phrase 'A language of flesh and roses' came into his head. But it would be a misrepresentation of the creative process if we took Spender too literally when he speaks of the phrase 'flashing' into his head. Why this phrase and not something else? Had the Gods selected his head alone to favour with this inspirational line? Nothing of the kind. When we unpack the mediations which preceded this phrase it should become clear that scores of people sharing these experiences and background knowledge could have arrived at a similar result, and, moreover, that the nature of the thought processes involved considerably narrowed down the range of poetic lines available to Spender. This is how Spender (1970, pp.68-9) traced out the sequence of his thoughts:

The industrial landscape which seems by now a routine act of God which enslaves both employers and workers who serve and profit by it, is actually the expression of man's will. Men willed it to be so, and the pitheads, slag-heaps and the ghastly disregard of anything but the pursuit of wealth, are a symbol of modern man's mind. In other words, the world we create - the world of slums and telegrams and newspapers - is a kind of language of our inner wishes and thoughts. Although this is so it is obviously a language which has got outside of our control. It is a confused language, an irresponsible, senile gibberish. This thought greatly disturbed me, and I started thinking that if the phenomena created by humanity are really like words in a language, what kind of language do we really aspire to? All this sequence of thoughts flashed into my mind with the answer which came before the question: a language of flesh and roses.

It is possible that from a strictly logical standpoint Spender's reasoning process may be flawed. But it is definitely a reasoning process, the end of which might have been reached by a number of socially aware poets on that train journey, sharing the same interest in language, and bearing in mind the fact that poets speak as frequently of roses as scientists do of test-tubes. There is nothing mysterious about the generation of the above phrase; what matters most is that the phrase emerged out of the system of mediations described by Spender. Were he an unemployed collier seeking work in the Black Country, the sight of a landscape dotted with factories and pitheads might have produced an idea inspired by a different system of mediations.

The Creative Product

If, as Sparshott and others argue, creativity is not to be found in the search for a creative process existing independently of creative work, then attention should focus on the creative work itself. Ian Jarvie (1981) draws an important distinction between creativity as a property of the creative work and creativity as a property of the creative mind. It is the latter, he says, which is trundled out in anecdotes. But creative work, he says, belongs to the public, objective and logical realm, of Popper's World Three. A similar endorsement of the conceptual priority of the created product is made by Larry Briskman (1981,p.135) who argues that if we cannot infer creative products from theories about creative personalities then inferences about creativity should be made from created products.

That is, the person is a creative one and the process was a creative process only in the light of our prior evaluation of the product itself as a creative product. If this is correct, then it follows that a scientific or artistic product is not creative *because* it was produced by a creative person or creative process, but rather that both the psychological process involved, and the person involved, are deemed to be creative *because* they succeeded in producing a product deemed to be creative. It is the creativity of the product which has, so to speak, logical priority.

At first sight Briskman's formulation merely moves the question back a stage. If we cannot identify creativity in a subject how can we identify it in the created object? Briskman's answer is that we can do so only by reference to *other* prior artistic and scientific products: 'a work of art or a scientific theory does not...wear its creativity on its sleeve'.(ibid,p.136) On Briskman's terms the rejection of psychological explanations of creativity must entail a demand for wider-ranging criteria than those employed to determine the quality of the created object. Briskman's criteria for determining a creative product is as follows:

1.   It must be a novel product, yet relative to the background knowledge entailed in previous products.

2.   It must put this novelty to a desirable purpose by solving a problem which is relative to that background.

3.   It must do so in a way that actually *conflicts* with part of this background, and accordingly improve or supplant it.

4.   Finally, it must be favourably evaluated; it must meet standards which are part of the prevailing background.

These criteria can be summarised by saying that a creative scientist or artist is one who produces a transcendental product. But more than this, the product must be seen to transcend the producer. In this context Briskman (ibid,p.150) refers to Haydn who, 'listening for the first time to his *Creation*, broke into tears and said: "I have not written this"'.

Reconstitution

Briskman's account of creativity transcends the narrow parameters applied to psychological accounts of the creative process. But it is equally important that the impact of the product on the relevant community is taken into consideration. Value is not strictly inherent in the product but in the social processes of endowment. The same forces that recognise creativity can withdraw that recognition, or even transfer what is deemed to be creative to another dimension of the product. As Briskman notes, the relationship of the product to the background knowledge is of fundamental importance. But the relationship between product and background knowledge is not merely a case of the product emerging out of background knowledge. This relationship is dynamic. Changes in the background knowledge may in turn be responsible for a reconstitution or re-evaluation of the status of the product. This would, in part, explain the transcendental nature of the creative product. A shift in interpretation or mode of representation may render a product in an entirely different light, reconstituting the original meaning bestowed by the producer. Augustine Brannigan's (1981) case history of the career of the Piltdown Man provides an excellent illustration of reconstitution - all the more so because of its manifold reconstitutions since Brannigan's account was published.

The Piltdown Man

In the *Origins* and subsequently in *The Descent of Man* Darwin developed his speculations on the common evolutionary roots of man and the higher apes. At the time of his writing only fossil remains of the Neanderthal Man (1857) had been uncovered. This, however, was a very advanced speciman, resembling modern man. So Darwin postulated a missing link. The first important discovery in the search for the missing link in Europe was the Mauer Jaw of Heidelberg Man in 1907. It was ape-like in the chin area but the teeth were human in form. On December 18th. 1912, Arthur Smith-Woodward and Charles Dawson announced the discovery of the 'Dawn Man of Piltdown', as a predecessor of the Mauer Jaw. This find included a large section of skull-cap and one side of a lower jaw. The proximity of the other remains in the area facilitated an estimate that the Piltdown remains were from the Pleistocene epoch, which was thought to be at least 200,000 years ago. The most striking feature was a large skull, concordant with a well- developed brain. But the jaw was thick and ape-like whilst the two molars were flat and human-like. Nevertheless, this discovery was expected given the background Darwinian theory, since the earliest human would be a blend of man and ape. What is more it was very much wanted

17

in that it provided British scientists with a lead over their German rivals. Britain had its own 'missing link'. Firmly convinced of the relatedness of the skull-cap and jaw Woodward not only announced a new species but a new genus, *Eoanthropus dawsoni*. (Dawson's Dawn Man)

There were several initial objections regarding the status of the discovery. Whilst the skull size was impressive some experts were puzzled by the primitiveness of the jaw. It was suggested that it might not belong with the skull; that it was an ape's jaw that had been washed down into the Piltdown quarry site from an earlier deposit. Woodward met these objections, arguing that the molars were peculiar to man, and he predicted that if and when a canine eye-tooth was found this would show human development, for it would not protrude above the level of the other teeth as it does in other simians.

In 1913 Woodward and Dawson had their confirmation when Teilhard de Chardin, working with Dawson, found the all-important eye-tooth close to the spot where the lower jaw had been disinterred. All doubts were dismissed. A great scientific discovery had been made, fulfilling expectations based on Darwinian theory.

Of course several anomalies remained and others soon came to light. Around 1936 a whole series of new discoveries of pithecanthropine man were made in Africa, China and Java. And a more advanced species, the fire-making, tool-using, cave-dwelling, Peking Man, was discovered. But unlike the Piltdown Man these discoveries on the very early ancestry of man suggested very human jaws with more primitive skulls. If the Piltdown discovery were correct it would follow that two separate lines of evolutionary development had occurred: on the one hand there would be Piltdown Man, with a large skull and ape-like jaw, and the others. Needless to say, the archeological community were unsettled by this matter.

In 1949 Kenneth Oakley, together with two anatomists, Joe Weiner and Wilfrid Le Gros Clark, tested the Piltdown remains with a newly discovered dating process. The results were staggering. Both jaw and cranium were found to have such low levels of flourine build-up that they were estimated to be no more than 50,000 years old, which suggested that Piltdown Man was a late Ice-Age curiosity and, since he post-dated some earlier forms, could be of no use in explaining their development. Further investigations, including a barrage of chemical, physical, and anatomical tests, on all the artifacts, revealed by 1953 that Piltdown Man was a forgery. Oakley and his colleagues determined that the jaw had been taken from a modern female orangutan and stained brown with chromium; the canine had likewise been obtained from a recent orangutan, but had been filed flat and painted with Vandyke brown paint; the molars were ape molars filed flat and dyed with chromium. Although the skull proved to be late

Ice-Age, it too had been dyed like the other artifacts. It was clear that the forgery could not have been done after the excavation without the knowledge of Woodward and others, so it was believed to have been perpetrated before the 'discovery'. Facts emerged which suggested to Oakley that Dawson, the amateur paleontologist eager for social enhancement, who had first uncovered the fossils, had engineered the entire fraud. This was partly corroborated by the fact that after his death no further finds were made at the Piltdown site. Over a dozen other candidates for the fraud have since been proposed, including Sir Arthur Conan Doyle and Teilhard de Chardin.

One important question has to be asked. Why was the scientific community so late in recognising the fraudulent nature of this alleged discovery? According to Brannigan the reconstitution of the Piltdown event, from discovery to fraud, was bound up with a change in the expectations of the scientific community. In 1912 the Piltdown discovery was not only expected according to Darwinian theory; it was also wanted by British scientists caught up in nationalistic rivalry with their German counterparts. By 1936, in the light of other discoveries, it had become an embarassing anomaly, and by the 1940's the further discovery that it was a fraud was expected.

But this was not the end of the matter. In 1972 Ronald Millar reopened the case by suggesting that it was not a fraud but a hoax. Millar (1972) dismissed the theory that Dawson had engineered the find. His character profiles of those associated with the Piltdown remains indicated that none were consistent with forgery. But he did suggest that Grafton Elliot Smith, who examined the original fragments and had the reputation of being a prankster with supercillious colleagues, may have pulled off a hoax that went too far, and was taken too seriously by the scientific community for him to own up. Millar's book contains an intriguing photograph of Grafton Elliot Smith and the other 'discoverers' examining the remains which, in the light of Millar's evidence, reveals a mischievous look in Smith's face.

To this day no single account is conclusive. Brannigan draws attention to a tape recording made by Professor Douglas, who died in 1978 having held the chair in Geology at Oxford. On the tape-recording Douglas suggests that the forgery had been concocted by his former teacher and predecessor, Professor W.J.Sollas. Apparently, Sollas had been slighted at a professional meeting, over his synthetic reconstruction of a primitive skull early in the century, by none other than Smith-Woodward. Sollas had removed a primitive skull from its stone casting by grinding away materials from around the bone. He then made models of the original bone, followed by more grinding until more bone was uncovered. After months of painstaking labour Sollas's reconstruction was dismissed by Smith-Woodward as a 'mere toy'. In his account of the incident Douglas maintains that Sollas was so enraged that he planned the Piltdown hoax in revenge. He had assumed that the hoax would be instantly recognised and that Smith-Woodward would have been a laughing stock. He had further assumed that the elephant's tusk, left with the other artifacts and modelled in the shape of a cricket bat, would have added to the humour - suggesting that the earliest Briton played cricket. But the joke backfired and Smith-Woodward was knighted.

Brannigan's account of the career of the Piltdown Man was published in 1981. It records a great discovery, later reconstituted as a fraud and later as a hoax. Concluding his contribution to the story Brannigan (ibid,p.141) said:

> This new interpretation, like the previous claim, objectifies a shifting corpus of elements, transforming the relevance of the past details in the light of present knowledge at hand. Just as the original Piltdown Man was seen as fulfilment of Darwin's prediction (which raised its own problems), so too the recognition of fraud solved other problems brought about by the validity of the Piltdown remains. Similarly the accounts of a hoax revise yet other details. Each successive interpretation brings a series of coherence to the details, though never with complete success.

The saga has nevertheless continued. In 1990 Caroline Grigson introduced further evidence which reimplicated Charles Dawson as one of the perpetrators of what she perceives as a fraud. This new evidence emerged during her research on the career of Sir Arthur Keith, Conservator of the Museum of the Royal College of Surgeons from 1908 to 1933. Grigson suspected that 'two classes of baddie' were involved; the actual perpetrator and those who knew or suspected, but kept quiet about it through fear of ridicule or dismissal from their posts. She also offered a further reason why the scientific community were not too rigorous in their initial investigation. This was bound up with institutional rivalry between the two great museums of London at that time; the Museum of the Royal College of Surgeons and the Natural History Museum. For whilst the former had a prestigious collection of human material the latter desperately 'needed a spectacular find of its own'.(Grigson,1990,p.57) This is not to say that they perpetrated the fraud, but rather that they were in a 'state of mind to accept any fossil hominids with a rather less than critical eye'.(ibid,p.57)

Grigson's case against Dawson is built around several visits he made to Sir Arthur Keith in October and November of 1913, when he examined the teeth of a female gorilla. Dawson made drawings and wax models of specimens in order to demonstrate to Smith-Woodward that 'the wear on the newly discovered canine was correct for an ape-like tooth'.(ibid,p.57) Grigson points out how the speciman Dawson used was abnormal and that his drawings were based on incisors and canines from an animal that had lost the first two molars from the lower side of the jaw and were consequently more worn than normal. Yet Dawson never mentioned this abnormality to Smith-Woodward. Grigson also refers to earlier visits by Dawson to the Royal College in 1913 and asks whether it is 'possible that Dawson made his drawings not in the autumn of 1913, but earlier that year - at the time when the canine was being prepared for discovery?'(ibid,p.58) Grigson's case may be inconclusive but it is plausible to suspect Dawson, who had good knowledge of the local geography, skills in modelling, appreciated the scientific community's desire to find the fossil man and knew what evidence would meet with acceptance on an anatomical basis. But he would need the help of an accomplice. Here Grigson introduces F.O. Barlow, the preparator in the geology department of the Natural History Museum who, under Smith-Woodward's direction, had made the reconstruction of the skull. 'Is it possible', asks Grigson,(p.58) 'that Barlow, such an expert modeller, treated much of the forged material after it arrived at the Museum, and made casts of the forged fragments without noticing anything amiss?' And even if he were not initially involved in the forgery he had a financial stake in maintaining the deception. Scientists had to pay expensively for Barlow's casts, which were in such demand, at two guineas for the skull and one for the jaw, that very soon the trade was being handled by a firm of professional fossil dealers in Weymouth. Even as late as 1941, though retired, Barlow was still selling casts. Grigson hints at a possible relationship between Dawson and Barlow; suggesting that it was possible for Barlow to have known and kept quiet, but she also suggests that 'he may have been the skilled accomplice that Dawson needed'.(ibid,p.58)

In the most recent, though certainly not the final chapter, of the Piltdown saga, suspicion falls upon Sir Arthur Keith as a collaborator with Dawson. Keith's knighthood and Fellowship of the Royal Society for his theories on human evolution were largely dependent upon the Piltdown evidence. According to a study by Frank Spencer (1990), which is based on unpublished archival research by Ian Langham who died in 1984 before publishing his work, not only did Sir Keith have the knowledge and material required to manufacture the remains, he had much to gain professionally from the discovery. Moreover, when questioned in 1953 after Oakley's revelations, Sir Keith seemed confused about his first meeting with Dawson and contradicted his published account which recorded their first meeting in 1913 after the discoveries. Spencer suggests that Sir Keith had concealed the fact that he knew Dawson prior to the 'find' and that he knew more about the site and the remains than he should have known before December 1912. Sir Keith is also known to have been the author of an anonymous article, published in the *British Medical Journal*, which contained information which should have only been known by Dawson, Smith-Woodward and their closest colleagues. According to Dr Chris Stringer (1990), Head of Anthropology at the Natural History Museum in London and keeper of the Piltdown fossils: 'Langham and Spencer's research have provided the best case yet assembled for the identity of Dawson's assumed collaborator. They have shown that nearly 80 years after the event it is still possible to find something new amongst the vast collection of Piltdown archives'.

Yet within a week or two after the publication of Spencer's research his claims were challenged by Lord Zuckerman (1990), former chief scientific advisor to several British Prime Ministers. Zuckerman put forward claims regarding whom he saw as a 'much more likely suspect ... Martin Hinton, an enthusiastic and somewhat eccentric individual who joined the Natural History Museum in 1910 as a "voluntary worker", and later rose to become keeper of zoology, a post he held until he retired in 1945'. (Zuckerman, 1990, p.16) According to Zuckerman's sources Hinton, whom he describes as 'a charming eccentric and good company', either alone or with others set out to make a fool of Smith-Woodward whom he had come to dislike during the two years he had spent as a voluntary worker at the Natural History Museum. Among the evidence supporting Zuckerman's allegations against Hinton is the latter's entry in Who's Who in 1935 which records his interest in hoaxes. Hinton's posthumous entry also lists a 'study of many hoaxes including the loch ness monster'. For Zuckerman the Piltdown artifacts are the work of a jocular hoaxer, not a serious-minded fraudster. With a new culprit even the role of the cricket-bat can be re-told. A letter in the New Scientist (Estling, 1990, p.67) records an earlier account by Harrison Matthews (1981) who claimed that in 1915 Hinton was so exasperated with the gullibility of the experts that he carved a piece of an elephant's leg-bone into the shape of a cricket-bat and planted it near the site. But even this failed to make Smith-Woodward look silly who simply pronounced it as 'a supremely important example of the work of paleolithic man'.

The Significance of Reconstitution

One of the primary reasons for regarding the discovery process as an irrational activity is an unwarranted fascination with a significant moment or major event, experiment or discovery. It is because creativity cannot be located in such a way that it is associated with mysterious powers. Attempts to focus on the creative product help to restore the possibility of a rational assessment of creativity, but any such assessment must acknowledge the context in which the work acquires significance. The account of the Piltdown Man reveals how the significance of these remains, at any stage in the process, is neither dependent upon the original discoverers nor on the objects themselves, but is to a certain extent bound up with the reconstituting nature of science and the transient expectations of the communities concerned with the product. The Piltdown discovery is now regarded as either a fraud or a hoax, according to the weight of evidence in either direction. The continuing saga provides an instance of what Nickles (1988) describes as a dynamic self- reconstructing aspect of science, according to which science continually transforms itself by re-working its previous results to create more objective accounts.

Reconstitution is not merely the effect of historical reappraisal where greater or less significance is given to certain data by historians in the light of fresh theory and information; it is part of the very nature of science as a self-correcting enterprise to re-evaluate its past in the light of new and immediate problems. Both longstanding and ill-structured problems are reconstituted such that, at a later stage, normal routine problem solving techniques can be applied. Later research reconstitutes both the problems and solutions. For these reasons fame is not a good indicator of creativity, as the products allegedly expressing creative genius are frequently reconstituted by successive contributions to the problem field. In contrast, most of the philosophy and history of science to date presents problems and solutions as static entities, but the reality is that they are constantly being reworked. The same experiments, theories and research, may turn out to be either crucial or irrelevant to later researchers, according to the context in which it is applied. On these terms some of the major transformations in the history of science may have different meanings to successive researchers than to those originally associated with them.

According to I.B.Cohen (1983, p.162) this view has implications for our understanding of scientific revolutions.

> All revolutionary advances in science may consist less of
> sudden and dramatic revelations than a series of
> transformations, of which the revolutionary significance may

not be seen (except afterwards, by historians) until the last great step. In many cases the full potentiality and force of a most radical step in such a sequence of transformations may not even be manifest to its author.

Whilst the bulk of scientific research is conducted within periods which Kuhn (1970) depicts as normal science, in many cases the revolutionary impact of a piece of research, experiment, or serendipitous event, may not be fully appreciated by scientists committed to or indeed limited by the paradigm of the day. Anomalies are frequently cordoned off or attempts made to reconcile them with existing canonical knowledge. For Kepler, working within a pre-Newtonian paradigm, the fact that planets have elliptical orbits was a 'necessary evil'. Yet his first law of planetary motion, when reconstituted, was of revolutionary significance from Galileo onwards.

Reconstitution occurs as a scientific programme develops. It is not merely a change in the meaning of scientific work perceived by either historians of science or even the way it is perceived by the scientific community at a later stage. There are also shifts in the meanings given to the work by the scientists's originally associated with it. This point is made in Jan Sapp's (1990) study of the changing significance of Mendel's experimental work in the 1860's.

> Throughout the twentieth century the significance of Mendelian genetics has changed. For example, the first generation of geneticists viewed Mendelism to be in direct conflict with Darwinian selection theory. By the 1930's Mendelism was held to be compatible with Darwinian selection theory. No doubt the meaning of many experiments can be continually reviewed as science proceeds. However, it is not just the meaning scientists place on Mendel's experiments that change with the development of Mendelian genetics, the inferences as to the meaning Mendel himself placed on the experiments also changes accordingly. (Sapp, 1990, p.149).

According to Sapp the Mendel legend, with its diversity of views concerning the alleged prematurity of his theories, the neglect of his work, the allegations of fraud and counter claims stressing his status as an exemplar of scientific method, are all indication of the power of rhetoric in scientific research. As a 'founding father' of genetics Mendel's 'true intentions' can be appealed to in support of conflicting claims over what concepts can be legitimately associated with Mendelian genetics. In this respect the meaning of Mendel's experimental work is reconstituted in the context of scientific disputes over what is intellectually acceptable to contemporary geneticists.

Reconstitution can best be appreciated against a model of scientific rationality which presents science as a mode of problem solving, or the exercise of curiosity. A strict external rationality would have no place for a problem shift. It should be stressed that science - when seen as a problem solving activity - is compatible with models of rationality which stress curiosity and play. Munevar (1989, p.485) stresses the role of 'curiosity and play with the world', but meaningful curiosity and play involves problem-solving, from the kitten whose problem is to free itself from a ball of wool to the physicist, like Feynman, taunting his colleagues with paradoxes and puzzles.

Properly understood the phenomenon of reconstitution reveals the limitations of heroic views of creativity as an irrational procedure beyond the scope of philosophical assessment. In the following chapters it will be argued that contrary to the beliefs of many philosophers, historians and practising scientists and artists, the processes of creativity, discovery and inventiveness, are fit subjects for philosophical analysis; that a rational account of the creative process is possible; that there is a case for saying it is a rational process, and that creative or innovative work is not dependent upon the proverbial star-studded genius whose powers defy explanation. It may turn out that artificial intelligence programs will never replace Michaelangelo and Newton, but this should not inhibit research into the nature of creativity and explanations of discovery.

Discovery and Justification: The Two-Context Distinction

The romantic affection for an irrational representation of creativity finds support not only in popular accounts of creative work but also in a distinction considered by many philosophers of science as essential to the very nature of scientific rationality: that is, the distinction between the context of discovery and the context of justification. In its modern form this two-context distinction can be traced as far back as David Hume in the eighteenth century and to F.C.S. Schiller in the early decades of the nineteenth century. The latter outlined differences between the logic of discovery and the logic of proof. In the seventeenth and eighteenth centuries there was little emphasis placed on any distinction between the two contexts, and attempts to construct a logic of discovery covered both aspects. Bacon, Descartes, Boyle, Locke, Leibniz and Newton, all believed it was possible to formulate rules which would lead to the discovery of useful facts. By the latter half of the nineteenth century this enterprise was dead. The logic of science was seen to be strictly concerned with the post hoc evaluation of well-formulated theories. The link was completely severed by William Whewell, whose denial of a logic of discovery anticipates twentieth century positivism. As Whewell (1847,pp.20-21) said: 'Scientific discovery must ever depend upon some happy thought, of which we cannot trace the origin; some fortunate caste of intellect, rising above all rules. No maxims can be given which inevitably lead to discovery'. Whereas earlier philosophers believed that only through a logic of discovery could theories be justified, from Whewell onwards it was argued that justification was not necessarily linked to discovery. Thereafter the central issue was the epistemological problem of justification and the logical status of already formulated theories. It should, however, be pointed out that Whewell's distinction between discovery and justification is not wholly representative of the hypothetico-deductivist approach taken up by twentieth-century positivists. As Andrew Lugg (1989) points out, Whewell is more of a foreshadow of Peirce and Hanson than the hypothetico- deductivist school. In his examination of Kepler's discoveries Whewell frequently refers to the context of discovery in terms of 'a succession of reasons, testings, choices abd exclusions'.

What began as a distinction between two contexts soon became an orthodoxy which ruled that discovery was excluded from philosophical concern. This can be seen in Augustus De Morgan's assertion that questions regarding the origins of an hypothesis are essentially unanswerable. 'The inventor of any hypothesis', he argued, 'if pressed to explain his method must answer as did Zerah Colburn, when asked for his method of instantaneous calculation. When the poor boy had been bothered for some time in this manner he cried out in a huff, "God put it into my head, and I will put it into yours"'. (De Morgan, cited by Passmore, 1968, p.124) According to De Morgan, and others following him, the role of the logician was exclusively that of testing already formed hypotheses. This trend has continued and more recent writers have reaffirmed the belief that a logical appraisal can only be undertaken with regard to judgements formulated in the context of justification. Under the influence of logical empiricism it was ruled that the logic of science was strictly a logic of justification. Consequently, one of the tenets of logical empiricism was a sharp distinction between the two contexts. Limiting their inquiries to the latter context the logical empiricists rarely found themselves critical of the popular accounts of discovery in terms of mysterious leaps into the unknown by God-like mortals whose powers defy explanation. In this sense a movement purporting to anchor philosophy to a scientific foundation preserved the belief that mystery and irrationality lie at the heart of the scientific enterprise.

The two-context distinction has two formulations; a logical one and an historical one.

1. It has been seen as a logical distinction between the psychological processes which occur when a scientist thinks up new ideas and the logical arguments which are concerned with the extent to which these ideas are supported by facts, consistency, or other evidential considerations.

2. It has been seen as a temporal distinction which separates accounts of what scientists do before they put forward completed hypotheses from accounts of what they do with them when they are developed.

Whilst there may be a case for maintaining these distinctions, in some form, the task of overcoming the rigid and dogmatic commitment to them is long overdue. The placing of discovery beyond the scope of methodological assessment reveals a misunderstanding of scientific reasoning and unnecessarily deprives the philosophy of science of any substantial content. To neglect philosophical investigation of discovery is not merely to neglect that part of science which most interests the scientist and lay-person; it is to ignore aspects of science which have a great significance for our understanding of rationality, epistemology and conceptual change. Similarly, to make a temporal distinction between the generation and application of hypotheses is incompatible with any serious historical investigation into scientific practice, as it ignores the processes by which the very anticipation of an outcome may have on the evolution of research.

The recognition that the processes which enhance discovery are amenable to logical analysis, and that discovery is a fit subject for philosophical investigation, would therefore provide a valuable step towards an understanding of creativity. However, it is important to stress that recent attempts to revive the logic of discovery are not analogous to the efforts of the seventeenth and eighteenth century philosophers. There is little enthusiasm for the attempt to equate a logic of discovery with a logic of justification. But what the 'friends of discovery' maintain is that there is a process of discovery which is both rational and amenable to philosophical investigation.

Problems With The Two-Context Distinction

1.   *It restricts the scope of philosophical investigation.*

Under the influence of Popper and Reichenbach the two-context distinction has been employed to determine the parameters of philosophical inquiry, according to which philosophers are confined to the examination of well-formed hypotheses and are not supposed to exhibit any interest in the creative business of discovering them. Consequently the process of discovery is held to be of interest only to historians, psychologists and sociologists. We are told by Reichenbach (1958,p.231) how: 'the act of discovery escapes logical analysis...it is not the logician's task to account for scientific discoveries...logic is only concerned with the context of justification'.

The same point is endorsed by R. Braithwaite (1953,pp.20-21): 'The solution of these historical problems involves the individual psychology of thinking and the sociology of thought. None of these questions are our business here'. But having been excluded from philosophy the context of discovery was not welcomed by the psychologists. For the first half of the twentieth century psychology was so much under the influence of Watson's naive behaviourism and a positivist orientation towards science that concepts essential to a scientific psychological appraisal of discovery, like imagination and creativity, were considered too elusive for legitimate scientific appraisal.

Such a view reflected the kind of timidity in philosophical investigation which has contributed to a separation between philosophy and interesting research in almost every branch of knowledge. But nowhere has this timidity been as damaging as in the philosophy of science: for a philosophy of science which cannot or will not address the problem of explaining scientific development is self-confessedly impotent and irrelevant.

Although logical empiricism is no longer dominant its distinction between discovery and justification is still brought out to block off any appraisal of the creative process. Popper, Carl G. Hempel, Braithwaite, Koestler, and many others unite in an insistence that the processes by which we come to have new ideas are qualitativly different to the processes for assessing them. Of course in one respect it is a harmless distinction. If it simply means that on some occasions we have new ideas and on others we submit them to tests, then it is true but uninteresting. If we were to say that the means by which the horse arrived at the two-thirty were distinct from the criteria employed to determine whether or not it actually won the two-thirty then we are still dealing with the trivially obvious. But if we cite this distinction to prove that whatever happened to the horse before the two-thirty has no bearing on how it came to win or lose the two-thirty, then we will have demonstrated complete ignorance of horse-racing. Yet this is exactly what Reichenbach, Popper and others have done in their respective accounts of scientific practice; they have limited rational conduct to one tiny aspect of scientific research.

In recent years Reichenbach's formulation of the two-context theory has been subjected to reassessment. It has been argued (Nickles,1980) that Reichenbach has been misinterpreted; that he only maintained that the distinction was a logical one, not a temporal one. On these terms criteria for justification could be applied at any stage in the process of discovery. Other exponents of the two-context theory have, nevetherless, outlined a temporal distinction.

2.   *It restricts the concept of rationality to only one aspect of scientific research.*

The thesis that discovery is amenable to rational analysis has not been popular this century. The prevailing view is that it proceeds by means of intuitive leaps. Exponents of the hypothetico- deductive (H-D) approach insist that scientific method consists in making observations, forming hypotheses to explain them, deducing consequences from these hypotheses, and then devising tests to either confirm or disprove the initial hypotheses. How hypotheses are reached in the first place is said to lie outside the scope of scientific methodology. Outlining the H-D method, Hempel (1966,p.15) argues that:

> The transition from data to theory requires creative imagination. Scientific hypotheses are not derived from observed facts, but invented to account for them. They constitute guesses at the connections that might obtain between the phenomena under study, and at uniformities and patterns that might underlie their occurrence.

Scientists often subscribe to this view. The physicist, Richard Feynman, (1967,p.156) said:

> In general we look for a new law by the following process. First we guess it. Then we compute the consequences of the guess to see what would be implied if this law we guessed is right. Then we compare the result of the computation to nature, with experiment to experience, compare it with

29

observation to see if it works. If it disagrees with experiment it is wrong. In that simple statement is the key to science.

The same point was echoed by Hermann Bondi,(1981,p.124) who saw imagination, not logic, as the most essential feature of discovery:

> The fact that you cannot deduce your scientific theory by any logical method shows that the vital part of the subject is originality and imagination. Formulating a scientific theory involves an imaginative leap.

When formulating the two-context distinction Reichenbach maintained that in the context of discovery a scientist conjectures and engages in thought processes in a non-rational manner, (here analogies with poetic inspiration are usually cited) but when the scientist wants to present finished work to a relevant community a 'rational reconstruction' is offered. It is this rational reconstruction that saves science from mysticism, argues Reichenbach, and it provides the philosopher with a subject matter. Says Reichenbach (1958,p.230):

> The scientist who discovers a theory is usually guided to his discovery by guesses; he cannot name a method by which he found the theory and can only say that it appeared plausible to him, that he had the right hunch, or that he saw intuitively which assumption would fit the facts.

Reichenbach's position is supported by the belief that whilst there is no algorithm for guaranteeing the prediction of major discoveries - and since these discoveries involve a radical break with the past - the processes in the context of discovery must be irrational. Pushed further this view sees the context of discovery lying beyond the scope of rational discourse, exemplyfying momentary mental experiences, 'aha' feelings and gestalt switches. The problem is that the very charge of irrationality aimed at the context of discovery can be equally made regarding the context of justification, for there are no algorithms to guarantee assertions in the context of justification.

3. *It restricts scientific rationality to a brief moment in the temporal process of discovery.*

If one accepts the distinction between discovery and justification there is a further requirment to see it as the boundary between the history and the philosophy of science respectively. Whereas the history of science is concerned with the facts surrounding the growth and development of science, philosophy is concerned with the logical structure of the finished research report. The historian has a growing body to observe; the philosopher dissects the corpse to see if the pieces are rationally assembled.

The first problem with this view is that if scientific discovery is considered too irrational to be investigated by philosophers then it should also be considered too irrational to be investigated by historians. For historical explanation has never been conceived of as a mere chronology of irrational events.

The second problem with this view is that it assumes that scientific activity can be chopped into neat sections. Yet understanding how scientists comprehend problems, react to them and solve them, is a crucial aspect of both the history and philosophy of science. Moreover, problem solving and having new ideas and testing them, takes place at all stages in the discovery process. And given that there is rarely ever a time when all aspects of a discovery are present for a finished research report - as further development is always possible - there is not really a time when the context of discovery can be located and isolated. To await the outcome of a final research report may take centuries, during which time all the important moves in the conceptual process are made. As J.N. Hattiangadi (1980) points out, Newton developed his views continually from his undergraduate days to the publication of the *Principia* in 1685. But at each stage of his work, from 1650 to 1700, a context of justification or evaluation can be discerned whilst the context of discovery cannot be given any temporal location. At best the context of discovery is only identifiable as the limits to justification.

Kuhnian Philosophy of Science and the Two-Context Theory

It was commitment to the distinction between discovery and justification, above all else, which provoked such a strong reaction to Kuhn and to the charge of 'mob psychology' which his critics made against him. According to Kuhn (1970) the bulk of scientific research is undertaken within the framework of what he describes as a 'paradigm' or central 'disciplinary matrix', wherein scientists share central presuppositions and theories and a common problem space. This he describes as 'normal science'. Occasional crises within the paradigm may initiate a period of 'revolutionary science' where the central presuppositions are displaced by those appropriate to another paradigm. (Throughout this text the expressions 'normal science' and 'revolutionary science' will be employed in conformity with Kuhn's characterisation of scientific development)

The charge of 'mob psychology' arises out of his thesis that there is no external rational yardstick whereby one can allegedly reason from one paradigm to another. Paradigms are said to be 'incommensurable' with one another. It would appear, from the standpoint of Kuhn's critics, that new paradigms are adopted by means of political and psychological persuasion or other influences - and Kuhn appears to reinforce this view by drawing analogies between sudden gestalt-switches and paradigm changes, and by drawing further analogies between political crises and social revolutions on the one hand with scientific crises and scientific revolutions on the other. At least on one occasion Kuhn virtually endorses Popper's view that imaginative insight rather than reason characterises the context of discovery. He says (1970a, p.12) that: 'we (himself and Popper) do not believe that there are rules for inducing correct theories from facts, or even that theories, correct or incorrect, are induced at all. Instead we view them as imaginative posits, invented in one piece for application to matters'.

On these terms some of Kuhn's critics have accused him of failing to address the question of discovery at all. Marx Wartofsky (1980,p.4) maintains that in one respect at least Kuhn lends support to the two-context distinction.

> Like other philosophers of science, Kuhn also left the nature of creativity in scientific thought untouched... Thus the logical empiricists, the Popperians, and Kuhn left the question of scientific discovery to one side. They assumed it, but none of them attempted to analyse it nor to explain it. In fact, like Polanyi, Kuhn left the process of scientific change to the domain of the non-rational, if not indeed the irrational. And at least in his earlier versions, Kuhn could speak of 'paradigm shifts' as 'leaps of faith', borrowing Kierkegaard's irrational concept here from the philosophy of religion. Such an account, therefore, does not deal with how discovery or innovation in scientific thought comes into being, but only with the process of how such discoveries come to be accepted; how they come to be believed after they have been introduced.

The charge of irrationalism is, to a certain extent, justified with reference to Kuhn's early accounts of incommensurable paradigms and gestalt-switch models. But the charge that his account leaves discovery

32

insufficiently explained is not strictly accurate. For Kuhn's account of paradigms which generate a commonly shared problem space does indicate how innovation in scientific thought occurs: scientists react to a clearly identified problem as presented by the paradigm which, admittedly, also defines what will count as a solution to the problem. Paradigm based science therefore offers a definite structure for the initial stages of solution generation, even if the problem space is later transformed and reconstituted by further developments in the process of discovery and shifts in the expectations of the scientific community It was not Kuhn's failure to provide an account of discovery, but rather his alleged failure to provide an account of justification, that upset his critics. For if the prevailing paradigm provides both the problem space and criteria for solutions there appears to be no grounds for a logic of justification which could override claims forwarded within any particular paradigm. Consequently Kuhn's account of the manner in which scientific change occurs appeared to ignore the distinction between history and logic, creating an impression that an explanation of how a thing arrived is equivalent to an explanation of why a thing was adopted. The problem was that Kuhn was closer to reality than his critics: as any Victorian father knew well; an explanation of how the infant arrived had a great deal to bear on the question whether it was to be adopted or not.

To advocate blurring the distinction between the genesis of a theory and its adoption may sound like an invitation to commit the genetic fallacy - confusing the truth of a statement with its origins. However, it should be stressed that the truth is not at issue here. Because the grounds for adopting H are not necessarily grounds for asserting the truth of H, the line between the origins of a statement and its adoption does not parallel the line between its origin and its truth. In any case few versions of the logic of justification make ultimate truth claims about propositions employed in the context of justification. It may well be that the reasons for adopting H are the same as those for suggesting H in the first place. Furthermore, if it can be said that an examination of the origins of a statement does have a bearing on its adoption, then it is perfectly rational to investigate them. And even if it is the case that the origins of some discoveries are more amenable to psychological or sociological investigation then this should not provide grounds for the exclusion of philosophical assessment. Psychology and sociology should then complement philosophical investigations of discoveries, rather than supplant them.

The business of philosophy of science is to understand how science works, and there should be no prohibitions on the means of achieving this understanding, even if it means looking into the minds of scientists, their social and economic backgrounds, their dietary interests, and, if necessary, their laundry lists. It has been pointed out by David L. Hull (1988,p.27) that 'the chief weakness of the logical empiricist analysis has been the emphasis of its advocates on inference to the near total exclusion of everything else about science, especially its temporal and social dimensions'. These other aspects were simply dismissed as 'irrelevant' to the truly philosophical aspects of science, although no philosophical reasons why were ever produced. It meant that philosophers were limited to modest activities, such as 'the analysis of rationality as such, the abstract relation between theories and data, and the like'.(ibid,p.27) On these terms investigations into the discovery process were deemed unphilosophical. But even if it were the case that discovery is primarily a psychological or sociological phenomenon this should not prevent philosophers from utilising material from these disciplines and from crossing the mythical barrier to avail themselves of developments in various branches of learning in the way that they have done with mathematics.

The following chapter will examine the arguments of philosophers who have adressed the problem of discovery, but it will concentrate on those who portray the genesis of creative ideas as an irrational activity. Chapter III will then examine the arguments of philosophers who have advocated a logic of discovery.

II Irrationalist conceptions of discovery

Irrationality and Hypothesis Generation

The popularity of irrationalist theories of discovery is illustrated in both biographical and autobiographical reconstructions. A typical example is the account of a crucial stage in the development of nuclear physics. In 1934 Enrico Fermi discovered that a beam of neutrons can destabilize the nuclei in a target more effectively if the neutrons are first slowed down by passing through a moderator. Fermi and his colleagues were conducting a series of experiments involving neutron bombardment when he discovered that when a layer of paraffin and other hydrogenous substances were inserted between the target and the neutron source levels of activity were affected in the target. It was inferred that neutrons rapidly lose their energy by repeated collisions with hydrogen nuclei, slowing them down and eventually reaching energies corresponding to thermal agitation. This discovery led eventually to the splitting of the atom. As Fermi said:

> We were working very hard on the neutron induced radioactivity and the results we were obtaining made no sense. One day, as I came to the laboratory, it occurred to me that I should examine the effect of placing a piece of lead before the incident neutrons. And instead of my usual custom, I took great pains to have the piece of lead precisely

machined. I was clearly dissatisfied with something. I tried every 'excuse' to postpone putting the lead in its place. When finally, with some reluctance, I was going to put it in its place, I said to myself, 'No: I do not want this piece of lead here; what I want is a piece of paraffin'. It was just like that: with no additional warning, no conscious prior reasoning. I immediately took some odd piece of paraffin I could put my hands on and placed it where the piece of lead was to have been. (Fermi, cited by Kneller, 1978, pp.110-111)

Examples of this kind lend support to the logical empiricist claim that the context of discovery is non-rational and that scientists do not reason to hypotheses but only reason from them. Yet even a superficial reading of this account raises glaring questions. Why did Fermi depart from his usual custom and have the lead precisely machined? Why postpone putting the lead in its place? What was the piece of paraffin doing in his laboratory? Why the paraffin and not any other piece of material? Why not put an odd piece of rag or a newspaper in the place where the lead should have been? If nuclear scientists really proceeded in such a haphazard way, trying anything that popped into their heads without any understanding why, then a serious accident would be the most likely outcome. George F. Kneller (1978, p.111) is highly sceptical of such an irrationalist account.

But this view is almost certainly mistaken. First, it is an empirical claim with no evidence to support it. Second, even if, at some point in the process of invention the scientist must rely on intuition, at other points he may be guided by rational considerations for which rules can be provided. Third, though there may not be a strict 'logic of discovery', there almost certainly are natural principles or 'rules of strategy' that scientists follow in formulating and pursuing hypotheses. These rules may be codified and formulated as an explicit rationale of discovery. Fourth, and most importantly, intuition, so called, probably is the condensation of one or more lines of rational thought into a single moment of insight.

Hypothesis-generation follows a logical structure, whether or not the subject responsible for the hypothesis is consciously aware of it. 'No one', says Kneller,(ibid,p.112) 'claims that because a deductive argument is grasped in a moment of insight, the argument has no logical structure'. What is frequently portrayed as a moment of irrational intuition is merely the tip of the iceberg; the reasoning process has either been subconscious or forgotten. This point has been stressed by Jules Henri Poincare when, after recounting a couple of dramatic flashes of inspiration, he observed:

> These sudden inspirations...never happen except after some days of voluntary effort which has appeared absolutely fruitless and whence nothing found seems to have come, where the way taken seems totally astray. These efforts then have not been as sterile as one thinks; they have set agoing the unconscious machine and without them it would not have moved and would have produced nothing. (Poincare , 1952, p.38)

Yet many philosophers of science and indeed many historians reject the view that hypothesis generation is rational. In the following survey of theories of discovery, which include those held by Popper, Polyani, Feyerabend and Koestler, these key assumptions unite different perspectives: that creative thought is essentially non-rational, and that whilst there may be disagreements as to how one reasons from hypotheses the business of reasoning to them is non-rational.

Popper

Sir Karl Popper can hardly be described as a mystic, or even an intuitionist. He has gone to great lengths to defend the view that science is a rational enterprise. He has gone to even greater lengths to distance himself from logical positivism. Yet his account of scientific discovery places him squarely within both camps. Borrowing Reichenbach's formulation of the two-context distinction Popper maintains that only the context of justification (or falsification), where completed hypotheses are presented together with provisions for their possible falsification, is of interest to the philosopher. There can be no question of analysis of the creative process. Popper's major work, *The Logic of Discovery*, reveals that he has done what few authors ever achieve: he has produced a book which denies any reality to the contents suggested by the title. Anyone hoping to find anything in it about the logic of discovery will surely be disappointed. It would be like acquiring a guidebook about New York only to find out, on reading it, that the author is convinced that there is no such place. Popper's (1977,pp.31-2) entire discussion of the logic of discovery is worth quoting at length.

> ...the work of the scientist consists in putting forward and testing theories.

37

The initial stage, the act of conceiving or inventing a theory, seems to me neither to call for logical analysis nor to be susceptible of it. The question how it happens that a new idea occurs to man - whether it is a musical theme, a dramatic conflict, or a scientific theory - may be of great interest to empirical psychology; but it is irrelevant to the logical analysis of scientific knowledge. The latter is concerned not with *questions of fact* (Kant's *quid facti?*), but only with questions of *justification or validity* (Kant's *quid juris?*)...
Accordingly, I shall distinguish sharply between the process of conceiving a new idea, and the methods and results of examining it logically. As to the task of the logic of knowledge - in contradistinction to the psychology of knowledge - I shall proceed on the assumption that it consists solely in investigating the methods employed in these systemic tests to which every new idea must be subjected if it is to be seriously entertained... my view of the matter, for what it is worth, is that there is no such thing as a logical method of having new ideas, or a logical reconstruction of this process. My view may be expressed by saying that every discovery contains 'an irrational element', or a 'creative intuition', in Bergson's sense. In a similar way, Einstein speaks of the search for those highly universal laws...'from which a picture of the world can be obtained by pure deduction. 'There is no logical path', he says, 'leading to these...laws. They can only be reached by intuition, based on something like an intellectual love (*Einfuhlung*) of the objects of experience.

According to Popper, in the genesis of scientific discovery reason must give way to faith.

I am inclined to think that scientific discovery is impossible without faith in ideas which are of a purely speculative kind, and sometimes even quite hazy; a faith which is completely unwarranted from the point of view of science. (ibid,p.38)

It is clear that for Popper the genesis of discovery is a matter only for psychological inquiry. Whilst the appropriate tests for the falsification of a conjecture may be carried out by ordinary mortals, armed with ordinary standards of rationality which can be handed down by teachers of logic from generation to generation, the business of conceiving a hypothesis is mysterious, even occult. In this respect Popper's account of discovery is in full conformity with romantic beliefs in the mystique of genius which find expression in biographical accounts of creative flashes, dramatic insights and serendipitous events. Despite his professed commitment to rationalism, Popper's account of discovery is highly irrationalist. His distinction between discovery and justification ultimately matches the traditional distinction between emotion and reason. Whereas the creative act relies upon emotional intuitions the logic of falsification rests on principles of reason.

In *Objective Knowledge* (1972) Popper formulated an evolutionary model of scientific development whereby a version of Neo- Darwinism functioned as an effective analogy with scientific development. On these terms both the amoeba and Einstein shared similar approaches towards problem-solving. Said Popper (1972, p.242): 'Problem-solving always proceeds by the method of trial and error: new reactions, new forms, new organs, new modes of behaviour, new hypotheses, are tentatively put forward and controlled by error elimination'. In this context Popper speaks of both Einstein and the amoeba employing methods of 'almost random or cloud-like trial and error movements' which are 'fundamentally not very different'. (ibid, p.247) The main difference, said Popper, was that 'Einstein, unlike the amoeba, consciously tried his best, whenever a new solution occurred to him, to fault it and detect an error in it'(ibid, p.247) whereas the amoeba presumably just gets on with whatever amoebas do. The approach taken by Popper is primarily one which has no place for a rational process of solution generation; rationality only comes on to the scene when known errors are rejected. Even when Popper rebuts the charge that his method of trial and error operates 'with completely chance-like or random trials' his account of rational regulation is in terms of 'after-effects', or of learning from mistakes. (ibid, p.245) Such a view reduces the history of science to a brute force search through immense space, guided only by hindsight derived from accidents. Behind this absurdity is an implicit view that in the absence of absolute certitude all hypotheses stand initially on an equal footing.

It is well known that Popper's reputation for rationalism, his crusade against dogma, rests on the principle of falsification according to which the hallmark of a genuine scientific enterprise is the potential falsification of conjectures. Genuine science, he argues, differs from dogmatic pseudo-science insofar as the former eschews claims to absolute certitude. Given his belief that all propositions are ultimately conjectural then it is rather surprising that Popper is strongly committed to the two-context distinction, as ultimately statements made in the context of justification are as equally contingent as those made in the context of discovery. Moreover, if as Feyerabend (1987, p.10) points out, 'good justifications have to be discovered just like good theories or good experiments', then good falsifications too, would belong to the context of discovery.

Popper's denial of a logic of discovery, however, should be seen as a reaction against Baconian inductivism and those who have espoused fail-safe mechanical methods of making discoveries. Nevertheless, the fact that Popper and his followers deny the existence of any fail-safe methods of justification has not, suprisingly, led them the banish the logic of justification to the provence of historians and psychologists.

There are two obvious ways in which an attack on Popper's position can be developed. First, one can develop the view that reason is and ought to be the slave of the emotions and consequently stress the primacy of emotional factors in both the contexts of discovery and justification. The second approach is to insist that both the contexts of discovery and justification are amenable to rational analysis. In line with the first option Michael Polanyi, Paul K. Feyerabend and Arthur Koestler stress that irrational factors are operational in both contexts, whilst pursuit of the other option can be seen in the paths taken by Charles Sanders Peirce, Norwood R. Hanson, Herbert A. Simon, and Kenneth Schaffner, who treat discovery as a process which is amenable to rational analysis. In the following sections we shall consider the first option in an examination of irrationalist accounts of discovery. In subsequent chapters various rationalist accounts will be examined.

Polanyi

In his major contribution to post-positivist philosophy of science, *Personal Knowledge*, (1958) Polanyi criticises those philosophers of science who are not interested in discovery but focus entirely on verification or justification. Despite their interest in inductive reasoning they reveal little interest in applying it to the context of discovery. He says:

> Philosophers deal extensively with induction, but when they
> occasionally realise that this is not how discoveries are made,
> they dispose of the facts to which the theory fails to apply by
> relegating them to psychology. (ibid, p.14, note)

Noting the reluctance of philosophers to study the context of discovery Polanyi outlined two methods by means of which they dispose of it. The first method is the relegation of discovery to psychology. This, as we have seen, is Popper's approach. If there are no rules for making new discoveries, argues Popper, the context of discovery is of no interest to philoscphers. (Precisely why discovery should be taken up by psychologists is not explained by Popper.) The second method for disposing of the context of discovery is by misrepresenting it. Armed with their distinction between inductive and deductive reasoning several philosophers have sought to capture the essence of scientific discovery but have only succeeded in distorting it. Bertrand Russell provides a classic example of what Polyani sees as a caricature of the process of generating new ideas. According to Russell, (1937, p.58) scientists proceed 'from observations of particular facts to the establishment of exact quantitative laws, by means of which future facts could be predicted'. On these terms there are three stages in the articulation of a scientific law:

> the first consists of observing the significant facts, the second in arriving at a hypothesis which if true would account for those facts, the third is deducing from this hypothesis consequences which can be tested by observation. (ibid, p.58)

This threefold process can be illustrated with a very simple example:

1.   One wakes up one wintry morning and hears the crunch of vehicle wheels over snow and ice. (Observation of significant facts)

2.   One infers that it has been snowing and that the snow has turned to ice. (Formulation of hypothesis)

3.   If this inference is correct the streets, rooftops and possibly the window sill should be covered in snow. (Deduction)

Having completed the reasoning process one can now go to the window, look out and observe whether the facts confirm the hypothesis.

Polanyi offers a radically different sequence to that presented by Russell. Essential to Polanyi's account are the following stages:

1.   A scientists first recognises a problem,

2.   then the scientist develops a personal obsession with the problem until

41

3.   a sudden flash of intuition or an imaginative leap provides
        the solution.

However, because the solution might not conform with existing rules and
expectations it may not be possible to test it for years.

The key to Polanyi's account of discovery lies in the notion of a
'personal obsession' with the problem. When Russell speaks of
'first...observing significant facts' he gives no account as to what makes
those facts significant. But for Polanyi the significant facts are determined
by an aesthetic sense and a personal obsession with the problem. This is
crucial, also, to his account of 'tacit knowledge'. For what is to count as
evidence depends on the very nature of the puzzlement felt by the scientist
confronted with a problem. Says Polanyi (1958,p.30):

> To select good questions for investigation is the mark of
> scientific talent, and any theory of inductive inference in
> which this talent plays no part is a Hamlet without a
> prince...Things are not labelled 'evidence' in nature, but are
> evidence only to the extent to which they are accepted as
> such by us observers.

On these terms one of the essential features of great discoveries is the
selection of significant facts or evidence that would have formerly been
considered insignificant. But what makes the facts significant to the
problem in the first place? This is where the personal element comes to
the fore. Polanyi's criterion of significance is bound up with a personal
sense of aesthetics which textbooks and rulebooks cannot provide. For
example, textbooks may explain the rudiments of X-ray photography and
various disease processes which can be detected by X-rays. Yet medical
students may have to struggle for weeks before they can see the significance
of shapes in an X-ray photograph. This knowledge is not provided in
textbooks; it belongs to that aesthetic domain which Polanyi depicts as
'personal knowledge'. One has to care about the kind of problems under
observation and it is this caring which governs the significance of what is
observed. A vetinary surgeon who cares about horses may place greater
significance on facts which a colleague, using the same textbook, might
ignore, and consequently stand a better chance of making an accurate
diagnosis. A motor mechanic with a personal interest in engines, and cares
about the craft, may be in a better position to solve problems related to
engine maintenance than one who merely follows the rule-book. This
aspect of personal knowledge is connected with one of the great paradoxes

of contemporary society; scientists, technicians, designers, programmers and craftsmen, are all expected to put aside personal interests and approach their respective disciplines in an objective manner. But if Polanyi is correct such an approach is counter-productive in that it restricts the emergence of those novel solutions which are bound up with a level of close personal involvement.

Instead of Russell's naive empiricism and Popper's doctrine of creative conjecture (embrace all now and test later), Polanyi offers a criterion for the selection of significant facts according to personal feelings governed by aesthetic canons. In *Personal Knowledge* he did not claim that aesthetic approval is equivalent to the kind of proof required in the context of justification; he maintained that it was simply a guide for significant observations in the context of discovery. Nevertheless, Polanyi did have serious reservations with the two- context distinction and in a paper called 'The Creative Imagination' (1981) he questioned its sharpness in the context of a critique of Popper's logic of falsificationism. Polanyi argued that Popper's account of the assessment of scientific theories offers little advance over logical empiricism, as ultimately falsification is as equally indeterminate as verification. Whereas Popper's logic of falsification rests on the assertion that a single piece of contrary evidence may refute a generalisation, Polanyi (ibid, p.91) maintained that experience only presents us with apparent contradictions, and that 'there is no strict rule by which to tell whether any apparent contradiction is an actual contradiction'. Moreover, despite Popper's claim that no scientific theory can be conclusively verified, Polanyi argued that we bet our lives on the correctness of scientific generalisations, particularly those underlying medicine and technology. Thus rejecting Popper's logic of falsification, Polanyi drew attention to the personal and 'emotional qualities' of a scientific system, the appeal to which cuts accross the boundary between discovery and justification. The appeal of a research programme, like Copernicanism, as in subsequent successful scientific revolutions, lay in its emotional attractiveness. Copernicus' followers, argued Polanyi, were emotionally attracted to the programme. That explains why it was adhered to despite resistance from exponents of the highly successful and practically useful Ptolemaic system which had been integrated into Western cosmology, metaphysics and religion for centuries. When making discoveries, argued Polanyi, scientists are governed primarily by aesthetic considerations, by 'hidden intuitions of coherence' which not only influence the results they are likely to accept but also the strategies they are likely to pursue. In the context of discovery, he says, 'the imagination sallies forward, and intuition integrates what the imagination has lit upon'.

(ibid, p.102) The function of 'creative intuition' is equally uppermost when one is assessing a discovery. Thus:

> the final sanction of discovery lies in the sight of a coherence which our intuition detects and accepts as real...history suggests that there are no universal standards for assessing such coherence. (ibid,p.102)

Despite his criticism of Popper's logic of falsification and formulation of the two-context distinction, Polanyi ultimately subscribes to Popper's doctrine that there cannot be a rational method by means of which we can explain the process of discovery. We simply 'tumble to ideas', says Polanyi, they 'cross our minds', 'come into our heads', or 'strike us' or simply 'present themselves to us'. Polanyi (1966, p.4) rejected any attempt to give a rational account of scientific discovery stating that 'no rules can account for the way a good idea is found for starting an enquiry, and there are no firm rules either for the verification or the refutation of the proposed solution of a problem'. Polanyi transcends the distinction between discovery and justification only at the expense of a rational account of scientific practice. Yet despite his irrationalist standpoint his remarks about 'personal involvement' and his account of 'tacit knowledge' are suggestive of a more accurate representation of scientific rationality than the H-D account in the sense that they provide a rudimentary guide to solution restriction and heuristic restraint. These aspects of discovery will be considered in more detail in chapters IV and V.

Feyerabend

Paul K. Feyerabend's alternative to the two-context distinction follows a roughly similar path to Polanyi. His case studies on the history of science, particularly his account of the success of Galileo's system over Ptolemaic astronomy and physics, are designed to promote the thesis that the boundaries of scientific rationality have been formulated in such a way as to exclude genuine scientific practice from serious consideration in the philosophy of science. Feyerabend's major contribution to the philosophy of science is his rejection of the search for eternally fixed rules of rationality and criteria for demarcation between science and other activities, which has failed to capture the development of science. The Popperian falsificationist methodology together with Imre Lakatos's theory of sophisticated falsificationism are criticised by Feyerabend (1975) as examples of a conflict between the restrictive rationality of the philosophers of science on the one hand and the rational conduct of scientists on the other. According to Feyerabend falsificationism not only fails to represent scientific practice but if it were ever seriously applied it would strangle at birth some of the greatest developments in science. The reason for this is that well-entrenched theoretical systems, such as the Ptolemaic Theory, have more arguments and proof on their side at the time of the appearance of their embryonic fumbling and inconsistent rivals, such as Copernicanism. In essence, Popperian falsificationism, if strictly applied, would prove to be incompatible with scientific practice where new theories frequently exhibit a sufficient level of tenacity to survive falsification.

Lakatos (1970) attempted to reconcile falsificationism with scientific practice. He proposed a weaker version of the doctrine according to which anomalies need not be held to falsify the theory until it is believed that the existing theoretical framework, or heuristic core, of a research programme is exhausted. What Lakatos described as a form of 'sophisticated falsificationism' embodied a doctrine of 'no falsification before a better theory'. (ibid, p.121)

Lakatos's theory of research programmes contrasted with the simple conjecture and refute approach of naive falsificationism. It also introduced a distinction between progressive and degenerative research programmes. In the former scientists may attempt to improve and modify existing theories rather than simply falsify the whole programme after each failure. As long as there are successes and there are no threats to the heuristic core, the programme is deemed progressive. If the anomalies persist and build up, or can only be removed by recourse to ad hoc assumptions which do not explain or introduce new facts, then the research programme is said to be degenerative.

The merits of Lakatos's approach are obvious in that it gives a much closer account of scientific practice than that found in Popper's naive falsificationism. But this success - as Feyerabend points out - is achieved at the cost of a degree of vagueness which destroys its ultimate claims regarding scientific methodology, as Lakatos does not provide any guidelines for drawing the crucial distinction between progressive and degenerative research programmes. Hence Lakatos, argues Feyerabend, simply abandons method.

In this respect Feyerabend poses a choice between the history of science and the logic of science, arguing that philosophers who pursue the latter, as it is currently understood, cannot deal adequately with philosophical problems arising out of the practice of science. Feyerabend is notoriously scornful of philosophers who employ the two-context distinction to block off studies in the history of science and interest in what are traditionally described as extra-scientific factors. He cites the following remarks by S.E. Luria (1985, p.125) as representative of the two-context theory:

> The model of the DNA molecule worked out by Crick and Watson stands on its own merits...The...story of how the DNA model was achieved, humanly fascinating as it may be, has little relevance for the operational concept of science.

Feyerabend (1987, p.110) acknowledges that 'most philosophers of science would agree' that only 'the context of justification explains its content and reasons for accepting it'. Nevertheless, he insists that science is not autonomous with respect to either the genesis or justification of its products. Knowledge, he argues, is an open ended 'living discourse', which is exemplified in recent pure mathematics where workshops, conferences and seminar meetings 'do not merely add information to the content of textbooks and research papers, they explain this content and make it clear that it cannot stand on its own two feet'. (ibid, p.111) For Feyerabend (1975, p.141) there is no essential difference between discovery and justification because 'anything goes' in either stage. Thus:

> Galileo prevails because of his style and his clever techniques of persuasion, because he writes in Italian rather than Latin, and because he appeals to people who are temperamentally opposed to the old ideas and the standards of learning connected with them.

But despite Feyerabend's rejection of the logic of falsificationism he nevertheless shares Popper's irrationalist concept of discovery.

> It is clear that allegiance to the new ideas will...be brought about by means other than arguments. It will...be brought about by *irrational means* such as propaganda, emotion, *ad hoc* hypotheses, and appeal to prejudices of all kinds. We need these 'irrational means' to uphold what is nothing but blind faith. (ibid, p.154)

Whereas Popper locates faith and inclinations in the context of discovery, Feyerabend (ibid, pp.155-6) proclaims their centrality in both contexts.

> What our historic examples seem to show is this: there are situations when our most liberal judgements...would have eliminated an idea or a point of view which we regard today

as essential for science...The ideas survived and they *can* now be said to be in agreement with reason. They survived because prejudice, passion, conceit, errors, sheer pigheadedness, all the errors which characterise the context of discovery, *opposed* the dictates of reason...Copernicanism and other *'rational'* views exist *today only because reason was overruled at some time in their past*...Hence it is advisable to let one's inclinations go against reason in any circumstances, for science may profit from it.

According to Feyerabend, scientists normally behave, and ought to behave, at all times in the manner which Popper attributes only to the context of discovery. A methodology which actually embraces requirements for the context of justification would, if seriously implemented, strike a death blow to scientific research.

A determined application of the methods and criticism and proof which are said to belong to the context of justification, would wipe out science as we know it - and would never have permitted it to arise. (ibid, p.166)

Rejecting the theory-observation distinction, which was once the cornerstone of logical empiricism, Feyerabend's espousal of the theory-loaded character of data rules out the distinction between discovery and justification. Observation is determined by a theory whose criteria of justification and proof is self-determined. To put it more explicitly: conceptual advances in science contribute to a transformation of criteria for justification, and it is these advances which determine the relevant justifying observations. Thus Galileo's belief in the observational reliability of the new telescope was co-emergent with the new theory it was invoked to prove. Each new conceptual standpoint provides confirming criteria of justification and proof. Radically new theories transform both observational terms and objects simultaneously with their theoretical counterparts. Discovery and justification are simultaneous.

Yet despite his refreshing destruction of restrictive methodologies and concepts of rationality which bear no relation to rational conduct, Feyerabend has little to say with regard to the genesis of new ideas. He has not produced a theory of how discoveries are made. His case studies and arguments show us how they are not made; that is, new ideas do not develop - nor could they survive - within the requirements of creative conjecture and refutation.

Koestler

Arthur Koestler was one of the most popular writers on scientific creativity. Although he insisted, in full agreement with Popper, that the genesis of discovery is irrational, he nevertheless had a great deal to say about it. But he fully suscribed to the two- context theory.

> The verification of a discovery comes after the act; the creative act itself is for the scientist, as it is for the artist, a leap into the dark, where both are equally dependent on their fallible intuitions. (Koestler, 1981, p.15)

In the context of discovery, argues Koestler, there is no significant distinction between new ideas in either art or science. In both cases the process is beyond explanation, mysterious and inexplicable. Says Koestler:

> There are always large chunks of irrationality embedded in the creative process, not only in art (where we are ready to accept it) but in the exact sciences as well. (ibid, p.14)

For Koestler, creativity occurs in an irrational context because it involves a regression from precise verbal thinking to more primitive forms of visual imagery. Thus scientists or creative artists facing a blocked problem may regress to pre-verbal images. Hence:

> Creativity often starts where language ends, that is, by regressing to pre-verbal levels, to more fluid and uncommitted forms of mental activity. (ibid, p.14)

It is in these allegedly pre-verbal states that the creative mind combines previously unrelated structures in such a way that more emerges from the end product than that which was put into it. 'The history of science', says Koestler (ibid, p.2), 'is the history of marriages between ideas which were previously strangers to each other, and frequently considered incompatible'. Creative work is the result of novel combinations.

> From Pythagoras, who combined arithmetic and geometry, to Einstein who unified energy and matter in a single sinister equation, the pattern is always the same... The creative act does not create something out of nothing, like the God of the Old Testament; it combines, reshuffles, and relates

already but hitherto separate ideas, facts, frames of perception, associative contexts. (ibid, p.2)

Essential to Koestler's conception of a 'creative act' is his distinction between 'associative' and 'bisociative' thought processes. Associative, or orderly thinking, is conducted within the scope of the 'rules of the game'. Thus in an associative context it is important to be familiar with the rules. If, for example, the game is naming opposites, then utterances like 'black', 'cold', 'wide' and 'left', are expected in response to 'white', 'hot', 'narrow' and 'right'. But not all thinking operates according to such clear cut rules. The game of chess is played according to rules, but sometimes there are hopeless situations where the most subtle strategies will not be of any help. In such a context a desperate player may resort to more primitive levels of thought and arrive at an additional strategy which, when combined with conventional chess strategy, may be aimed at reducing the opponent's ability to perform adequately. Giving the opponent a jumbo-sized martini or placing a hypnotist in the audience, for example, would be a combination which brought a new dimension to the game. This combination of two distinct activities is what Koestler describes as an act of 'bisociation'. It combines two frameworks of rules. Bisociative contexts are those situations where an act of 'cross- fertilization' takes place which is characteristic of the 'sudden leap of the creative act', as distinct from 'the more normal, more pedestrian, associative routines of thinking'. (ibid, p.2)

But whereas associative thought processes are explicable in terms of known rules, Koestler's bisociative contexts are decidedly inexplicable. We can have no idea how the mind reached out for the new combination as in these contexts it descends into a pre-verbal or pre-rational dimension. But this is a rather misleading account of creativity. There are, at any stage in a process of dealing with problems, a limited number of acceptable combinations. In the chess example the only plausible combinations would be restricted to those which either enhanced one's own capacity to play or reduced one's opponent's capacity to play. Other combinations would be meaningless. Some proposals would be limited by the moral beliefs of the problem-solver, such as the combination of armed combat and chess where shooting the opponent would be unthinkable. Even the most radical, daring, immoral and illegal, combination will be to some extent bounded by the structure of the problem. The adopted combinations might not be strictly within the existing parameters of the game but they will be, in some sense, meaningfully related to problems generated within the game. Like Polanyi, Koestler's theory of creativity rests on a thesis of nonisomorphism, the view that it is only very rarely that the 'series of psychological events in the mind of the individual scientist leading up to the discovery of a theory can be represented in propositional form'. (Curd, 1980, pp.208-9) This is why Koestler stresses the non-linguistic nature of creative thinking. But even if this were true, and innovators did think in non-linguistic patterns, it would not rule out the possibility of a rational simulation of the thought processes leading to a discovery. Historians, biographers and contemporaries, are frequently capable of reconstructing the development of a theory with reference to bits of incomplete data, such as the author's correspondence, half finished research notes and other sources which are not set out in a coherent propositional form.

In a limited sense Koestler's distinction between associative and bisociative acts matches the distinction between normal and revolutionary periods of science formulated in Kuhn's (1970) *The Structure of Scientific Revolutions*. For the most part scientists proceed with a shared framework of rules and expectations but when the weight of anomalies produce a crisis or, as Koestler says, 'when the world moves on', there follows a period of 'fumbling and groping for that happy combination of ideas' which will 'lead to a new synthesis', (Koestler, 1981, p.4) or new paradigm. (Kuhn, 1970)

Nevertheless, the analogy between Kuhn and Koestler has limitations: whilst Kuhn stresses the historical structure of scientific discoveries Koestler, as we shall see, is primarily concerned with revelatory flashes of illumination. Notwithstanding these important differences, both Koestler and Kuhn are committed to the view that at least some discoveries - those in bisociative contexts (Koestler) and those which engender paradigm change (Kuhn) - are qualitatively distinct from other more pedestrian and routine discoveries, and are consequently not amenable to rational analysis. When Koestler describes creativity he does so in terms of those flashes of inspiration and other visual metaphors which abound in scientific and artistic biographies. Koestler refers to moments of creative insight in terms of 'Aha reactions', moments when bits of a puzzle suddenly and inexplicably click into place. This experience he compares with seeing the point of a joke - the 'Haha reaction' - which occurs when we combine two mutually exclusive contexts to create a comic effect. In science, says Koestler, the comic effect is transitional; it occurs when scientists ridicule a new combination, but ceases when the marriage of incompatibles bears fruit. Whereas 'comic discovery is the paradox stated; scientific discovery is the paradox resolved'. (ibid, 1981, p.5)

Koestler's account of bisociative acts provides neither an explanation of discovery nor a method by means of which discoveries can be generated. Bisociative thinking may take place but it cannot be considered as a useful generative device as it not rationally directed and involves nothing more than a brute force trial and error search. According to Koestler, so it would seem, there is no limit to the permissible combinations of different categories. Some combinations may yield discoveries, others humour, and others may yield sheer nonsense. Koestler recognises that only some marriages bear fruit. But if bisociative techniques are to be incoporated into a rational account of discovery, then a principle for juxtaposing different categories is required. As Eugene Laschyck (1986, p.166) points out: 'Juxtaposition without unifying ideas produces unrelated diversity, not a new unity'. The unification of terrestrial and celestial physics can be seen as a bisociation, but it was not a random process, nor was it a pre-verbal regression; it required the prior formation of ideas by means of which these respective phenomena could be reconciled. Novel ideas are not merely combinations; they involve novel ways in which categories are combined. A creative theory might be the product of a combination, but one first has to have the ideas that will facilitate recognition of the significance of the outcome, otherwise one is simply left with the standpoint of naive inductivism and the problem of deciding which, out of masses of observations and ideas, has the most significance.

Koestler has clearly said more about the context of discovery than Popper, and recognises that the more pedestrian 'associative' discoveries are amenable to rational assessment, but he has still left the question 'How does the bisociative act occur?' beyond explanation. We are left with nothing more than anecdotes about sudden flashes of illumination, eureka moments and 'aha' reactions. Perhaps the analogy with illumination is responsible for a great deal of confusion with regard to the nature of creative discovery. Koestler is not alone in placing great emphasis on metaphors of illumination with references to 'flashes of insight' thus conveying the impression that a discovery is a finite act which can be assimilated to a specific event. The reality is that discovery is a process which is more extensive than any particular experiences that may be had during its development. Discovery is not a momentary thing; it is a process in which both the object of knowledge and possibly several knowing minds interact over a considerable period of time. Yet in most of the literature on discovery it is assumed that discoveries occur at recognisable times by scientists who are fully aware of what was discovered. Against these assumptions and against his own occasional mentalistic accounts of discovery, Kuhn (1977) has demonstrated conclusively that major discoveries, such as the discovery of X rays and oxygen, cannot be given precise historical dates and that those associated with them were not fully aware of what it was that they has actually discovered.

Koestler is highly misleading about the nature of discovery when, in his influential work, *The Act of Creation*, he presents the 'eureka act' as the essential component of creative discovery. The following examples, cited by Koestler and many others in the irrationalist tradition, have become legendary among the anecdotes about creativity. The first is Henri Jules Poincare's account of his discovery of the Fuchsian functions.

> For fifteen days I strove to prove that there could not be any functions like those I have since called Fuchsian functions. I was then very ignorant; every day I seated myself at my work table, stayed an hour or two, tried a great number of combinations, and reached no results. One evening, contrary to my custom, I drank black coffee and could not sleep. Ideas rose in crowds; I felt them collide until pairs interlocked, so to speak, making a stable combination. By next morning I had established the existence of a class of Fuchsian functions, those which come from the hypergeometric series; I had only to write out the results, which took but a few hours...Just at that time I left Caen, where I was then living, to go on to a geologic excursion under the auspices of the school of mines. The changes of travel made me forget my mathematical work. Having reached Coutances, we entered an omnibus to go to some place or other. At the moment when I put my foot on the step the idea came to me, without anything in my former thoughts seeming to have paved the way for it, that the transformations I had used to define the Fuchsian functions were identical with those of non-Euclidean geometry. I did not verify the idea; I should not have had the time, as, upon taking my seat in the omnibus, I went on with a conversation already commenced, but I felt a perfect certainty. On my return to Caen, for consciences sake, I verified the results at my leisure. (cited by Koestler, 1975, p.115)

Here are all the ingredients of a dramatic flash in the context of discovery which involve a bisociative combination followed by verification in the context of justification. The second example is the account of a dream of Friedrich August von Kekule, Professor of Chemistry at Ghent in 1865.

> I turned from my chair to the fire and dozed...Again the atoms were gamboling before my eyes. This time the smaller groups kept modestly in the background. My mental eye, rendered more acute by repeated visions of this kind, could not distinguish larger structures, of manifold conformation; long rows, sometimes more closely fitted

together; all twining and twisting in snakelike motion. But look! What was that? One of the snakes had seized hold of its own tail, and the form whirled mockingly before my eyes. As if by a flash of lightning I awoke. (cited by Koestler, 1975, p.118)

Kekule's insight led to an important discovery in organic chemistry; the discovery of the structure on the benzene molecule which, as Koestler notes, is one of the cornerstones of modern science. Biographical reports such as this lend further support to irrationalist theories of discovery. Here the bisociative act is presented as a sudden inexplicable phenomenon. But are these discoveries beyond the scope of rational explanation? Cannot adequate reasons be given to show why Poincare and Kekule arrived at their respective discoveries? The element of irrationality is built into the description of the creative act. This, however, is a presupposition about discovery which illicitly creeps into descriptions. Undue emphasis is placed upon the psychological states which may occur at certain stages during a discovery process. It is important to realise that such creative feelings, however dramatically presented, do not in themselves constitute the discovery. It is extremely doubtful whether they are of any significance other than a source of anecdotal material for either entertainment value or as a means of giving a temporal location to a discovery in order to resolve a priority dispute. But the feelings described have no value in themselves. Eureka feelings may equally accompany discovery or justification. One can have a eureka feeling when discovering new theories or when rediscovering well-established theories. Every schoolboy is aware of that moment of mental exhiliration when he finally grasps a rather banal proof that his teacher has been trying to hammer into his head for weeks. There is nothing creative in this; it is simply an exalted state of mind. Equally so, one can feel the urge to shout 'Eureka' when one is completely wrong. Darwin (1925, p.83) once wrote: 'I cannot remember a single first-formed hypothesis which has not after a time had to be given up or greatly modified'. As a rule, anecdotes about creative flashes are only sought from successful scientists. There is little said about inventiveness that proved abortive, the dream that dissolved on waking, the flash of inspiration that accompanied an enormous howler, the 'got it' followed by the 'lost it', and the 'Aha' followed by the 'Oh no'! A flash of illumination is, at best, nothing more than a dramatic highlight within a larger process of discovery, and is usually mediated by the training, interests, and level of knowledge already attained by the creative mind. It is misleading to speak of the 'act of creation'. Discovery is a process which inevitably takes time with the outcome rarely transparent to the discoverer. For the most part the products of dreams are not plausible candidates for serious scientific development and tests. Any significant discovery has its origins in a rational context. Kekule's dream, which we are told, led to the discovery of the structure of the benzene molecule, was a contribution within a process of scientific development which may have begun with the discovery of benzene by Faraday in 1827 and achieved completion by 1890. Kekule's private thoughts, his moments of exaltation, were but a contribution to a scientific process against a background of problems to which he and others were attuned.

It may be the case that none of the steps in the reasoning process were articulated - as in the case of Poincare's discovery of the Fuchsian functions. But this is irrelevant to the argument's logic. They may have been ommitted from memory or taken subconsiously. Too often attention to insight is so exclusive that the logical steps by which that insight is reached are ignored. Kekule's dream of a snake biting its own tail solved his problem regarding the structure of the benzene molecule, but unless one can uncover a reasoning process from canonical knowledge to the novel conclusion, such an account would be of little service to science. We must be wary of exaggerated claims about this particular dream. On examination it is not surprising that he should have seen its significance. As Margaret Boden (1977, p.331) points out: 'Since chemists already expected a molecule's behaviour to depend on its shape, or spatial structure, and since the structures previously envisaged failed to exhaust even a very limited number of topologically distinct types, it is perhaps not so surprising as it is sometimes suggested that Kekule should have had this dream and recognized its significance'.

An inability to trace out the complete reasoning process in any given report of an illuminative flash may indicate nothing more that defects in the methods employed by historians and philosophers of science. It certainly provides no evidence for the existence of any occult creative process, just as our failure to explain creaking doors and things that go bump in the night cannot provide evidence for the existence of ghosts. On many occasions we may fail to observe steps taken in a sequence but this does not indicate their non-existence. When we watch the magician pull a rabbit out of a seemingly empty hat we do not conclude that he has effected a suspension of spatial and temporal continuity; we merely note our inability to observe the connexions which the magician has so skilfully hidden from the audience. It is similar with the accounts given by Poincare, Kekule and other examples of instant illumination cited by Koestler. Even when the flash heralds a so-called qualitative leap of the kind which characterises Koestler's bisociative context, there is good reason to infer the existence of an unconscous, subconscious, or semi-conscious, chain of inferences or pattern sequence which links the new standpoint with existing canonical knowledge. And if it were acknowledged that the reasoning process was subconscious, or even unconscious, this need not be deemed to be a concession to an irrationalist conception of discovery. There have been sufficient advances in psycho-analysis for it to be possible for therapists to trace out and explain various stages in subconscious thought processes. If so, then there should be no significant differences between conscious and subconscious thought processes involving creative discoveries. Any difficulties encountered in an attempt to trace out or detect a series of logical steps from the recognition of a problem to a novel solution should not be taken as necessary and sufficient evidence for the conclusion that they do not exist.

It has often been recognised that creative thinking may involve thought processes that are either partially or totally hidden from the creative thinker. This does not render them irrational or pre-verbal, nor does it suggest that the unconscious is the essential location of creativity. Henry James depicted the creative unconscious activity of the mind as 'the deep well of unconscious cerebration'. But this is merely a picturesque avowal of ignorance. Of much greater accuracy is Shaw's remark about Ibsen: 'The existence of a discoverable and perfectly defined thesis in a poet's work by no means depends on the completeness of his consciousness of it'. (cited by Clignet, 1985, p96) What Shaw had to say about the rationality of poetic composition can be equally applied to the generation of scientific theories.

Unconventionality

Appeals to unconventional life-styles are frequently made in support of irrationalist theories of discovery. Yet unconventional life-styles can be immediately discounted among the factors essential to the generation of creative ideas. Kant was a paragon of conventionality in his lifestyle but was eminently creative. Prisons are full of unconventional characters who will never be creative. A great deal of unconventional behaviour is useless and tiresome. Moreover, unconventionality is determined by cultural factors which are subject to change. Newton lived a conventional life and like many of his contemporaries he believed in demons, which by twentieth-century standards would be unconventional.

Having discounted unconventional life-styles the inquiry here will be restricted to a more promising field; unconventional solutions to specific problems, for an unconventional orientation to a problem is frequently associated with creative discoveries. Changes in sets of heuristics (seen in scientific revolutions) are often associated with discoveries involving a different and, perhaps, an unconventional orientation to the subject. Very often the initial thoughts of radical innovators are regarded as an outrage against commonsense. Yet the surprising move is the one which is held to provide a solution to an otherwise impossible problem. Philosophers and scientists too, have maintained that such counter-intuitive procedures are essential to scientific progress. Nevertheless, it must be stressed that the unconventionality which often accompanies creativity should not be confused with the creativity itself. An unconventional approach may be necessary for the generation of a new heuristic framework, but it is never sufficient. For if unconventionality were sufficient then lunatics would be creative, and the net effect would be the limitation of scientific progress to a blanket trial and error search. This is precisely the problem with appeals to radical unconventionality - advice to abandon all restraint. It simply means that heuristics are to be jettisoned for a speculative and possibly lengthy trial and error search.

Unconventional solutions to problems produce an element of surprise. But on close examination it is possible to draw a distinction between surprise as a response to mere unconventionality - aberrant behaviour - and the surprise generated by an unconventional, but satisfactory, solution to a problem. The latter is described as 'effective surprise'. (Bruner, 1967, p.3) The content of surprise may vary according to the kinds of activities people engage in. But effective surprise, generated by a serious solution, is not in response to the outlandishness of the proposal or even its rareness. Effective surprise has the quality of being both important and initially obvious, and the shock of recognition is experienced by a prepared mind. There is a quality of self-evidence in effective surprise, as expressed in great formulae such as the formula for the conservation of energy and the 'stunning condensation of all falling bodies into Galileo's $S = g + {}^2$ is of this order'. (ibid, p.3)

As subfields of unconventionality, madness or periods of insanity, are frequently associated with tales of creative discovery. Yet despite the popularity of madness, divine possession, or the effects of hallucinagenic drugs - from Plato's *Ion* to the Romantic poets and beyond - there is no satisfactory link between these unfortunate states and creativity. An elegant disavowal of these kinds of explanation is found in Chekov's remark that anyone who has claimed to have written a story 'without premeditations' can rightly be called a lunatic. Likewise Kekule's account of his discoveries as instant illuminations should not overshadow the fact that he was an indefatigable worker, known to his friends as a 'walking encyclopaedia', who drove himself hard to the detriment of his health in later life. And despite claims about the influence of drugs on Coleridge, neither the *Ancient Mariner* nor *Kubla Khan* would have emerged without months spent immersed in the literature of travel. Similar preparation can be seen in the work of Melville whose scholarly research into the history of whaling preceeded his writing of *Moby Dick*. After exhaustive inquiries Goethe concluded that there are less than forty distinctive tragic situations within which even the most unconventional plot would be confined. Once the limits of possible variation are recognized what matters most is not an unconventional rejection of the rules but an intelligent use of them. Meaningful and effective unconventionality demands a painstaking familiarity with existing knowledge; the surprise of creative unconventionality is mediated by the accumulation of conventional facts.

It takes time to develop the kind of recognition skills that major scientific figures are alleged to possess when they make crucial observations. Chess grand masters are said to possess about 50,000 chunks of information in long term memory. This would take about ten years of professional training. But what of geniuses? According to Herbert Simon (1981, p.108) 'except for Bobby Fisher, who reached grandmaster status in nine years and some months from the time he began to play chess, there is no record of anyone achieving that level in less than a decade'. The same can be said for music and the other arts. 'Unless we except Mozart, there is no record of a composer producing first-rate music before he had completed a decade of serious study and practice; and even in the case of Mozart the music that he composed between the seventh and tenth years after he began writing is notable as Mozart juvenilia rather than the music of a grandmaster. (ibid, p.108)

Any serious appraisal of a problem should limit the scope of unconventionality. For if the innovative thinker has no criteria to govern the solution, and no means of limiting the generation of clues out of the research, then the activity is meaningless. What is required when confronted with 'stuckness' - or a restricted heuristic - is not a return to the open-mindedness of brute force trial and error, but the replacement of an inadequate hypothesis generator with a more fruitful one. What matters is not that the solution is unconventional, but that the heuristic which replaces the old one is more successful in that it is more relevant to the problem at hand. Thus in chess the novice is effectively surprised when his opponent demolishes him with a surprising move like the sacrifice of a queen. For the novice is trained to reject moves that directly involve the loss of important pieces. But the secret of the opponent's success is not in the unconventional nature of the move, but in the fact that she is familiar with an additional strategy that guides her to more promising solutions. Unconventionality only yields greater productivity if the problem solver has an appropriate new heuristic to supersede the old one that has restricted her predecessors. In this context it is necessary to outline the fundamental difference between the crank and the serious innovator. Superficially they are similar insofar as their approach to the problem is unconventional. The differences quickly emerge when we see the crank persisting with an unconventional strategy which bears less and less relation to the problem - or indeed any problem of note - whilst the serious innovator, armed with a superior heuristic, goes on to modify and even transform the entire research field.

Free Wheeling and Brainstorming Techniques

Beliefs in the irrationality of hypothesis generation underpin several schools of thought which promote psychological strategies for the production of new ideas. Of dubious value are methods which emphasise the overcoming of mental blocks which allegedly inhibit the free flow of ideas. Behind such strategies there often lies a hotch-potch of ill-conceived beliefs about the mysterious and irrational nature of the creative process, backed up by accounts of instant illumination. On these terms rational restraints, regulative principles and accumulated wisdom, are seen as restrictive barriers rather than as means of enhancing a propensity to eliminate pre-doomed paths. Thus many text-books on creative thinking emphasise the need to overcome mental blocks, free the mind, expand consciousness, cast more light and remove critical restraints. The following remarks in J.F. Jackson's *The Art of Solving Problems* (1975, pp.121-122) are representative of textbook advice to suspend criticism in the context of discovery:

> Once the ideas begin to flow, a certain kind of creative momentum develops which helps to prevent our critical faculties from coming into operation and producing an inhibitory effect. This is sometimes called 'free-wheeling'. To keep this momentum up we must be prepared to put forward ideas which normally we would regard as unrealistic or even ridiculous. This principle is closely related to the avoidance of criticism and the suspension of judgement, both of which have a powerful influence on the momentum of the flow of ideas.

Central to the free-wheeling technique is the two-context distinction, according to which criticism is reserved only for the context of justification. There is here, also, a quasi-mystical account of the 'flow' of ideas which are not supposed to be structured, either by the problem or by the collective knowledge of those attempting to resolve it. Even unrealistic thoughts are encouraged.

A free-wheeling search is a random search; a wide shot which, like the monkeys typing out the works of Shakespeare in the British Museum, might hit the target, given enough monkeys and time. The same can be said of the brainstorming techniques developed by Alexander Osborn, psychology professor and consultant in industrial creativity. However, brainstorming techniques are marginally superior to free-wheeling techniques in that the former consists of sessions which are, at least, dominated by a specific problem. The idea is that a group discuss a problem, play back recorded tapes, and then eliminate whatever is later considered irrelevant. More sophisticated versions include a brainstorming technique developed by William J.J. Gordon of the Arthur D. Little Company, a research organization which would invent products on order for its clients. With the Gordon method only the chairperson of a group knows the exact nature of the problem. The rest of the group are then asked to discuss a general principle, but are gradually introduced to the problem itself. The idea of 'keeping them in the dark' is based on the belief that suspension of critical thought and expert prejudice is essential to the generation of ideas. In blissful ignorance of the complete problem members of the group allegedly retain flexibility of thought for longer periods.

The principle behind these techniques is that random generation of ideas produces more. But there is also an attempt to produce an element of fusion from a greater number of sources and in effect produce a setting in which Koestler's bisociative act can occur. The rules and guidelines for brainstorming are: 1) suspension of critical judgement; 2) quantity of ideas; 3) free wheeling, and 4) cross fertilisation of ideas. The method is simply that of achieving the widest shot possible. Although they have the advantage of generating more ideas through cross fertilisation developed in the session, without heuristics brainstorming techniques are primarily devices for brute force trial and error searches. And trial and error searches without heuristics are meaningless. However, in actual practice free wheeling techniques, brainstorming sessions and related methods of generating ideas, are guided by implicit heuristic devices which block off the more irrelevant ideas. Insofar as these systems work they do so in spite of their methodological underpinnings. Without heuristic restraint there is little chance of success with such random searches.

III   Can there be a logic of discovery?

The Historical Background

The tendency to exclude the context of discovery from rational inquiry has not always prevailed. As Kenneth Schaffner (1980, p.191) points out: 'the logic of scientific discovery and the logic of scientific justification have more than once traded prince and pauper status in the philosophy of science'. As evidence he cites Descartes who, in his *Rules for the Direction of the Mind*, believed he had provided a method for arriving at new knowledge which had demonstrative force. Similarly, Francis Bacon in *Novum Organum* expounded a theory of discovery which had no provisions for the distinction between discovery and justification. John Stuart Mill also recommended methods for the discovery of new knowledge and was criticised by his contemporary, William Whewell, (1968, p.286) who reflected the dominant trend when he said that 'a supply of appropriate hypotheses cannot be constructed by rule, nor without inventive talent'. Yet despite the prevailing views of the late nineteenth and most of the twentieth century, that discovery cannot be amenable to rational assessment, a minority have claimed that discovery does involve a logical process. Charles Sanders Peirce maintained that scientific discovery could be characterised by a mode of inference which he described as 'abductive' or 'retroductive' inference. Peirce's interest in the logic of discovery was not developed during the heyday of logical empiricism but was revived and given fresh impetus around the mid-twentieth century by Norwood J. Hanson, and more recently by Herbert A. Simon, Alan Newell, and other researchers in the computer sciences. This chapter will focus on the respective formulations of a logic of discovery by Peirce and Hanson, and on Peter Achinstein's criticisms of the retroductive model of inference.

Peirce

Although Peirce was a nineteenth-century contemporary of William James and John Stuart Mill he is a philosopher whose ideas belong to the last decade of the twentieth century, and is rightly regarded among the 'friends of discovery'. For Peirce, philosophy of science was not merely confined to procedures in the context of justification of theories; it was also concerned with the procedures by means of which they were obtained. As Jurgen Habermas (1972, p.91) says: 'What separates Peirce from both early and modern positivism is his understanding that the task of **methodology** is not to clarify the logical structure of scientific theories but the **logic** of the procedure with whose aid we *obtain* scientific theories'.

Like many recent post-positivist philosophers, Peirce emphasised that any context of discovery presupposed a level of background certainty. Rejecting the view that scientific discoveries emanate from irrational or random events he drew attention to the way in which data is presented to an inquiring mind in an organised manner. Without a pre-arranged system or plan, he held, nothing could be learned from nature. In an essay written in 1883, Peirce formulated some of his views regarding a natural aptitude for 'guessing right', which human beings must necessarily possess in order to accumulate knowledge.

> Nature is a vaster and less clearly arranged repertory of facts than a census report; and if men had not come to it with special aptitudes for guessing right, it may well be doubted whether in the ten or twenty thousand years that may have existed their greatest mind would have attained the amount of knowledge which is actually possessed by the lowest idiot. But, in point of fact, not man merely, but all animals derive by inheritance (presumably by natural selection) two classes of ideas which adapt them to their environment. In the first place, they all have from birth some notions, however crude and concrete, of force, matter, space and time; and, in the next place, they have some notion of what sort of objects their fellow beings are, and how they will act on given occasions. Our innate mechanical ideas were so nearly

correct that they needed but slight correction. The fundamental principles of statics were made out by Archimedes. Centuries later Galileo began to understand the laws of dynamics, which in our time have been at length, perhaps, completely mastered. The other physical sciences are the results of inquiry based on guesses suggested by the ideas of mechanics. The moral sciences, so far as they can be called sciences, are equally developed by our instinctive ideas about human nature. Man has thus far not attained to any knowledge that is not in a wide sense either mechanical or anthropological in its nature, and it may be reasonably presumed that he never will.

Side by side, then, with the well-established proposition that all knowledge is based on experience, and that science is only advanced by the experimental verification of theories, we have to place this other equally important truth, that all human knowledge up to the highest flights of science, is but the development of our inborn animal instincts. (Peirce, 1983, pp.180-1)

The above passage clearly commits Peirce to one of the fashionable nineteenth-century theories of instincts. But it should be appreciated that he was not merely looking for a principle to reduce the development of human knowledge to the level of instinctive feelings. On the contrary, his appeal to 'animal instincts' and his references to an aptitude for 'guessing right' should be taken as a recognition of mechanisms responsible for the selection of the most plausible explanations of puzzling phenomena. Moreover, Peirce's view that the mind is somehow attuned to the structure of the physical universe has found a modern form of expression in David Bohm's theory of implicate order.(Bohm and Peat, 1988)

According to Peirce a methodology of science should fulfill one basic requirement, namely to show that the methods advocated have a reasonable chance of finding interesting and satisfactory theories. He therefore took account of the fact that out of an infinite number of possible solutions to a problem scientists only operate with a few. For Peirce this indicated that an early stage in a discovery was some kind of process for filtering out the less plausible hypotheses.

It was important to Peirce that knowledge must be seen to develop out of puzzlement. The fairly obvious point that knowledge progresses in response to novelty has not always been appreciated by epistemologists. This is because so many epistemological investigations have concentrated primarily on the faculties of cognition, rather than on the problem-oriented contexts in which knowledge is operative. Traditional epistemologies were also misleading when they evaluated the status of passive sensation reports, such as 'I see a chair' or 'that is a red object', as possible candidates for the foundations of scientific certitude. Scientific knowledge is not passively acquired; it involves an interaction between a prepared mind, reality and other minds. It develops out of attempts to solve problems. To respond to a problem involves a presupposition that enough knowledge is already held for one to be puzzled about it. Furthermore, one can only be said to be in the grip of a problem if one either has an idea or belief concerning the kind of circumstances or situation that could resolve that problem. For Peirce (1968, p.143) the very essence of scientific inquiry was in the recognition of a problem.

> The inquiry begins with pondering these phenomena in all their aspects, in the search for some point of view whence wonder shall be resolved. At length a conjecture arises that furnishes a possible Explanation, by which I mean a syllogism exhibiting the surprising fact as necessarily consequent upon the circumstances of its occurrence together with the truth of the credible conjecture, as premises. On account of this Explanation, the inquirer is led to regard his conjecture, or hypothesis, with favour. As I phrase it, he provisionally holds it to be plausible.

Peirce recognised that when a scientist is confronted with a problem even the most tentative hypothesis will be selected according to rational criteria. Not all hypotheses can be described as 'credible conjectures'. Some are more of less credible than others, according to the climate of informed opinion, the level of scientific knowledge, physical and mental reality, and the surrounding milieu. To account for this process of selection Peirce outlined his theory of inference which he called 'abduction' or 'retroduction', whereby a scientist does not rely on chance, luck, or genius, putting forward whatever comes to mind, but acts selectively, advancing the most plausible conjecture.

> The first stating of a hypothesis and entertaining of it, whether as a simple interrogation or with any degree of confidence, is an inferential step which I propose to call *abduction*. This will include a preference for any one hypothesis over others which would equally explain the facts, so long as this preference is not based upon any previous knowledge bearing the truth of the hypothesis, nor on any

testing of any of the hypotheses, after having admitted them on probation. I call all such inference by the peculiar name, *abduction*, because its legitimacy depends upon altogether different principles from those of other kinds of inference. (Peirce, 1957, pp.236-7)

The existence of a criterion of selection among plausible hypotheses guarantees the role of reason in the process of discovery. Peirce's concept of 'abduction' differs from familiar concepts of deductive and inductive inference and refers to the kind of inference which takes place when scientists respond to anomalies. According to Peirce, deductive inference cannot yield new facts or truths, whereas an inductive inference involves a generalisation which must reach beyond the supporting evidence of its premises. He also recognised that one of the problems with inductivism, from Bacon onwards, was that the inductive method lacks a criterion of relevance: it does not provide grounds for deciding which facts should be collected. Now Peirce acknowledged that deduction and induction may be relevant to the confirmation of a completed hypothesis, but he maintained that the hypothesis is reached by means of this entirely different process of abduction. This term he derived from Aristotle's *'apagogue'* which Peirce understood to mean 'the acceptance or creation of a minor premise as a hypothetical solution to a syllogism whose major premise is known and whose conclusion we "find to be a fact"'. (Anderson, 1987, p.15)   Peirce does not give a comprehensive account of abduction, and his alternative use of the term 'retroduction' is suggestive of theoretical uncertainty. According to one view (Rescher, 1978) the term 'abduction' refers to the process by means of which hypotheses are formulated whereas 'retroduction' refers to the processes of eliminating the least favourable. On these terms retroduction - the later stage - would correspond to the logic of falsification which means that it is only Peirce's concept of abduction which offers an alternative to the hypothetico-deductive (H-D) method.   According to Nicholas Rescher (1978, p.42): 'The task of abduction is to determine the limited area of promising possibility within the overall domain of theoretically available hypotheses'. For Rescher abduction is the key to Pierce's logic of discovery, as it refers to the mechanism for the selection of the most plausible hypotheses in any given problem domain. It is, in some sense, the notion of plausibility which functions as the restraint on hypothesis generation. 'By plausibility', says Peirce, (1931-1958, 8, p.223) 'I mean the degree to which a theory ought to recommend itself to our belief independently of any kind of evidence other than our instinct urging us to regard it favourably... Physicists certainly today continue largely to be influenced by such plausibilities in selecting which of several hypotheses they will first put to the test'.

The concept of plausibility is clearly crucial to Peirce's account of discovery, but given that (according to Rescher's account) plausibility functions as a mechanism for eliminating hypotheses in the abductive phase there seems to be little point in maintaining a rigid distinction between abduction and retroduction. Both terms, it would appear, refer to processes of 'rule out' and hypothesis restraint. In any case throughout his widely scattered writings Peirce frequently used these two terms interchangeably.

Peirce's account of plausibility as a tool in the economy of research provides a more accurate account of the process of discovery than the blind generate and test approach offered by exponents of the two-context theory. But there is little in Peirce's account of abduction or retroduction of how hypotheses are actually generated. Although he stresses that the anomalous fact must be explained by the conjecture, he does not indicate any logical mechanism for generating the conjecture in the first place. Yet despite this neglect of a logic of generation, Peirce does indicate shortcomings in any approach to limit rational inquiry to either the confirmation or falsification of well formed hypotheses. For as Peirce recognised, the problem with the H-D method is that it is bounded only by the limits to the imagination, whereas in practice a scientist cannot, and certainly does not want to, test or even entertain every possibility. Some hypotheses are dismissed out of hand, or may never be allowed to emerge. Such examples of rational suppression are familiar in daily life; we frequently suppress sentences or thoughts which do not appear relevant to the problem at hand. Yet some suggestions carry an immediate ring of plausibility. It is the regulative role of the concept of plausibility which features prominently in Peirce's abductive or retroductive model.

It is a primary hypothesis underlying all abduction that the human mind is akin to the truth in the sense that in a finite number of guesses it will alight upon the correct hypothesis... For if there were no tendency of that kind, if when a surprising phenomenon occurred in our laboratory, we had to make random shots at the determining conditions, trying such hypotheses as that the aspect of the planets had something to do with it, or what the dowager empress had been doing just five hours previously, if such hypotheses had as good a chance of being true as those which seemed marked by good sense, then we could never have made any progress in science at all. But that we have made solid gains in knowledge is indisputable; and moreover, the history of science proves that when the phenomena were properly analysed... it has seldom been necessary to try more than two or three hypotheses made by clear genius before the right one was found. (Peirce, 1958, p.220)

Peirce's appeal to a rational procedure for the rejection of all but the most plausible conjectures has a decidedly modern ring, but he never developed his views with regard to the generation of plausible conjectures. Instead he referred to instincts, to the possession of commonsense, or 'horse sense', which humans share with other animals. Just as the chicken which successfully pecks through its eggshell does not waste its time on other activities, so argued Peirce, a scientist confronting a pressing problem cannot afford to waste time on endless hypotheses. Accordingly, Peirce's account of abduction or retroduction is more of a contribution to the economy of research than to the logic of discovery, as the latter requires an account of hypothesis generation. Moreover, the appeal to instincts is clearly unsatisfactory as a yardstick of scientific rationality, and is a poor candidate as a serious explanation of the discovery process. But if all reference to instinct is replaced with appeal to a method based on accumulated knowledge, research and background theory, then Peirce's contribution to the logic of discovery is decidedly important. However, there was little discussion of Peirce's model of abductive or retroductive inference until it was raised several decades later by Norwood R. Hanson.

Hanson

Throughout the 1950's Hanson almost singlehandedly argued the case for a logic of discovery. Maintaining that the context of discovery has a definite logical form he revived Peirce's retroductive method and argued that Popper, Reichenbach, and Braithwaite were fundamentally mistaken in their rejection of a logic of discovery. Says Hanson (1958, a.p.71):

H-D (hypothetico-deductive) accounts all agree that physical laws explain data, but they obscure the initial connection between data and laws; indeed, they suggest that the fundamental inference is from higher-order hypotheses to observation statements. This may be a way of setting out one's reasons for accepting a hypotheses after it is got, or for making a prediction, but it is not a way of setting out reasons for proposing it or for trying out an hypothesis in the first place. Yet the initial suggestion of an hypothesis is very often a reasonable affair. It is not so often affected by intuition, insight, hunches, or other imponderables as biographers and scientists suggest. Disciples of the H-D account dismiss the dawning of a hypothesis as being of psychological interest only, or else they claim it to be the provence solely of genius and not of logic. They are wrong. If establishing an hypothesis through its predictions has a logic, so has the conceiving of an hypothesis.

On these terms Popper's approach to the logic of discovery is incomplete. The exclusion of the context of discovery suggests that Popper's methodology is really a 'logic of finished research reports'.(Hanson, 1965) But what should a logic of discovery undertake? Hanson excludes two possible answers to this question. It is not, he says, a laboratory manual for making important discoveries. Nor is it a logician's symbolic restatement of the historical and psychological conditioning of great discoveries. Instead, a logic of discovery should concern itself with the scientist's actual reasoning which '1) proceeds retroductively *from an anomaly* to 2) the delineation of a kind of explanatory H which 3) fits into an organised pattern of concepts'. (ibid, p.50)

To appreciate Hanson's account of discovery it is helpful to contrast it with the H-D method, or method of creative conjecture, which is exemplified in Popper's version of the two-context theory. For Popper, as we saw in Chapter I, the question of how a scientist arrives at a new law or a new theory is not a matter for logical inquiry. There can be no inferences to theories, only inferences from them. For Popper (1965, p.192) theories are 'free creations of our own minds, the result of almost poetic intuition'. (The question whether poetry creation is as irrational as Popper thinks will not be considered here, although it might be suggested that if a particular poet cannot describe his work it may simply indicate that he is inarticulate.) In sharp contrast to Popper, Hanson (1958, b.p.1083) maintained that there was nothing in even the greatest scientific discoveries that could lend support to an irrationalist theory of discovery. Said Hanson: (1958, b.p.1083)

> To form the first idea of elliptical planetary orbit, or of constant acceleration, or of universal gravitational attraction does indeed require genius; nothing less than a Kepler, a Galileo, or a Newton. But this need not entail that reflections leading to these ideas are unreasonable, or a-reasonable. Perhaps *only* Kepler, Galileo, and Newton

had intellects mighty enough to fashion these notions initially. To concede this is not to concede that their reasons for first entertaining such concepts surpass rational inquiry.

Against the belief in the mysterious origins of discovery Hanson (ibid, p.1083) offers the following homily:

> H-D accounts begin with the hypothesis as given, as cooking recipes begin with the trout as given. In an occasional ripple of culinary humour, however, recipes sometimes begin with 'First catch your trout'. The H-D account describes a recipe physicists often use after catching hypotheses. However, the ingenuity and conceptual boldness which mark the whole history of physics show more clearly in the ways in which scientists *caught* their hypotheses, than in the ways in which they elaborated these once caught.

Whilst philosophers of science have been primarily concerned with how to set out reasons in support of a hypothesis once it is formed, Hanson attempted to set out reasons for proposing it in the first place. In this respect Hanson (ibid, p.1073) claims an affinity with Aristotle and Peirce: 'when they discussed what Peirce called "retroduction" both recognised that the proposal of an hypothesis is often a reasonable affair'. This is how Hanson (ibid, p.1073) formulates his position:

> One can have good reasons, or bad, for suggesting an hypothesis initially. These may be different from the reasons which lead one to accept the hypothesis once suggested; in some cases the two may be different in type. This is not to deny that sometimes one's reasons for proposing a hypothesis are identical with one's reasons for accepting it.

For Hanson there can be a logic of discovery but it is different to the logic of justification. There are reasons for suggesting an hypothesis and there are reasons for accepting it. The reasons for suggesting it are the logic of discovery and the reasons for accepting it are the logic of justification.

Reasons for suggesting and reasons for accepting

Most discussions of Hanson's proposals for a logic of discovery focus on his distinction between these two sets of reasons which he formulates as follows:

1.   the reasons for accepting an hypothesis, H, and
2.   the reasons for suggesting H in the first place.

Is there a difference between these two sets of reasons? For Hanson the reasons for accepting H were the reasons for believing H to be true. But the reasons for suggesting H were those which made it a 'plausible conjecture'. Thus:

> H will be accepted as true if repeated observations support H - if consequences of H used as predictions, confirmed H - if new phenomena are revealed through operations on H. Again, if H is compatible with, or derivable from, already established theories, this inclines us to accept H as true. (ibid, p.1074)

Self-evidently these conditions do not have to be met in full before formulating H as a plausible conjecture. When he turns to the reasons required for the suggestion of H as a plausible conjecture, Hanson points out that Kepler could not have supported his elliptical orbit hypothesis before the idea of such an orbit for Mars seized him as at least plausibly possible. Some of the reasons for the plausibility of Kepler's conjecture might have been represented as follows:

1.   Does H look as if it might be that from which well known phenomena P1, P2,...etc., could be shown to follow?
2.   Does H look as if it might explain P1, P2,... etc.?, (for some values of H the answer at any time would be 'no' - an answer for which good reasons could usually be marshalled). (ibid, pp.1074-5)

On the other hand the reasons might have been as Kepler reasoned in *De Motibus Stellae Martis*:

1.   Does the hypothesis of a non-circular orbit for Mars appear to be that from which it would follow that the planet's apparent velocities of 90° and at 270° of eccentric anomaly would be greater if the orbit were circular?

And

2. Does the hypothesis look as if it might *explain* the facts? (ibid, p.1075)

Quite obviously the above questions are relevant to Kepler's initial thinking, which was not based on a hunch plucked from the air. From the start Kepler believed that a careful study of the orbit of Mars would provide the key to planetary motion because its orbit was furthest from that of a circle: hence his reliance upon the observations of Tycho Brahe. In effect Kepler approached the problem armed with a level of background knowledge which clearly governed the space of plausible solutions. This is why Hanson rejected Braithwaite's (1953, p.20) suggestion that 'exactly which hypothesis was to be rejected was a matter for the "hunch" of the physicist'. In Kepler's case there were good reasons for rejecting some hypotheses outright. Other values of H - that Mars' colour was responsible for its velocity or that Jupiter's moons were responsible - would not have even appeared to Kepler as candidates for an explanation. And, if required, good reasons could be produced for not considering them.

It has been objected that there is something spurious in Hanson's distinction between reasons for suggesting H and the reasons for accepting H. Hanson (1958, b.p.1076) summarised some of the objections as follows:

> The only logical reason for proposing H at all is that certain considerations incline one to think H is true. Obviously these are the same conditions which (if substantiated) will ultimately lead one to accept H as true. The distinction Hanson advocates is at bottom merely psychological, sociological, or historical in nature; it says nothing of logical import about the difference between suggesting and establishing scientific hypotheses.

By way of a reply to this objection Hanson asks his opponent to consider as a general proposition H the general proposition that *all* planets have elliptical orbits. Kepler, he says, had many reasons to formulate and propose H, but one of them certainly included the limited one, H, that Mars' orbit is elliptical. And if its orbit is elliptical, then being a typical planet, its dynamical properties will be shared by other planets. Hence it is reasonable to propose H.

But these reasons would not establish the truth of H, says Hanson. All we have here is an analogy, and on Hanson's terms 'analogies cannot establish hypotheses, only observations can: in this the H-D account is correct'. (ibid, p.1077)

While inductive reasoning and analogies may provide reasons for suggesting a hypothesis, Hanson maintained that only observations are relevant to its acceptance. In the case of Kepler's elliptical hypothesis in order to establish H 'one must observe the positions of the other planets, determining that each could be plotted on a smooth curve whose equations approximate to those of an ellipse. When this is done it may be possible to assert H'. (ibid, p.1077) Thus contrary to Braithwaite's insistence that the reasons for suggesting H are psychological, Hanson can demonstrate that: 'Logically Kepler's analogical reasons for proposing H just after 1609 were good ones. But logically, they would not have been good reasons for asserting the truth of H - something which could be done confidently only years later'.(ibid, p.1077) In the context of the discovery, says Hanson, analogy is a good reason, although it is not sufficient for acceptance. Thus:

> If I say 'Jones has a good reason for H', that is contingently true, if true at all. Jones could have had other reasons for H. But this statement is logically different from 'A is a good reason for H'. What are and what are not good reasons is a logical matter ... Whether or not A is a good reason for H's proposal is purely a logical enquiry.(ibid, pp.1077-8)

Although Kepler's reasoning was analogical, other reasons could have been cited. In some cases a good reason to suggest H might be because one had heard it from a recognised authority. For example: 'Kepler's assistant, Bartsch, had a good reason for proposing H: it was that Kepler had proposed H'.(ibid ,p.1078) It is not unreasonable to follow an authority so long as there are not overwhelming reasons against so doing. There is nothing unreasonable about saying 'me too' when consensus has moved in a particular direction. Of course these kinds of reasons do not, in themselves, establish the truth of a proposition.

Yet Hanson's distinction between reasons for suggesting and reasons for accepting is unsatisfactory. He is right to assert that Popper, Reichenbach, and Braithwaite are mistaken in their insistence that deliberations in the context of discovery are irrational, or of psychological interest only, but his own formulation of the distinction raises problems. Whilst it can be acknowledged that one may have different reasons, or more reasons, for the acceptance of H than are necessary for the initial

71

suggestion of H, this does not commit one to a conceptual distinction between the two sets of reasons. Moreover, it is unhelpful to suggest that the reasons for accepting H are primarily observational. When Einstein replaced the classical Newtonian concept of gravitation as a force exerted mutually by bodies with the idea of gravity as arising from the purely geometric property of curvature his formulation had instant appeal. It was both elegant and simple, and provided Einstein with the key to a description of the spatial structure of the universe. But the hypothesis of analysing gravity as a property of space was not capable of yielding observational support, and in this sense is different to the context in which Neptune was hypothesised and then observed on the basis of Newtonian theory. Einstein's new formulation was more of a new conceptual scheme, or paradigm, for the interpretation of observational data, and accordingly it was adopted without observational confirmation.

Hanson's appeal to observational criteria for the acceptance of a hypothesis is clearly at odds with his general account of scientific inquiry, according to which there are no theory-neutral observations, and that observations cited as reasons for acceptance could be impregnated by the same theoretical framework which may have been responsible for the initial suggestion of the hypothesis. Hanson, it would seem, can only maintain his distinction between reasons for suggesting and reasons for accepting by ruling out observational statements made in the context of suggestion. But the recognition of, and description of, anomalous facts in the context of suggestion would also be ruled out. Furthermore, although one can distinguish between reasons for suggesting something and reasons for accepting something as true in many particular cases, it is just as difficult to provide a logical basis for this distinction as it is to provide one for the discovery- justification distinction that Hanson so rightly criticises. As Achinstein (1971, p.138) points out, Hanson fails to capture the distinction he seeks.

> Any of the reasons he mentions for suggesting a hypothesis can also be reasons for accepting it, though some will be stronger reasons than others. The fact that a hypothesis offers a plausible explanation of the data can be a reason for suggesting it, but it can also be a reason for accepting it. The fact that Mars travels in an elliptical orbit and that Mars is a typical planet can be a reason for suggesting that all planets travel in elliptical orbits. But it can also be a reason, though perhaps not a conclusive one, for accepting the hypothesis about all planets.

Achinstein's point is that 'whatever type of reason can fall under the first heading can fall under the second, and vice versa'.(ibid, p.139) For example, Brahe's data could be explained by the hypothesis that all planets move in elliptical orbits. This could be a good reason for either proposing or accepting the hypothesis. Reasons for suggesting and reasons for accepting need not be conceptually different; one might have more reasons, or stronger reasons, for accepting H which include the reasons for suggesting H. Moreover, deductive reasons, which fall within the logic of justification, may be employed as reasons for suggesting H. This, of course, is not to say that reasons for suggesting H and reasons for accepting H are necessarily the same on every occasion, but rather that there is no qualitative difference between the two contexts in which reasoning takes place.

If Hanson's appeal to a qualitative distinction between reasons for suggestion and reasons for acceptance is abandoned, does it follow that there is no basis for maintaining, in some form, distinctions which highlight different aspects of the discovery process? This question will be addressed in the final chapter when a range of modes of reasoning appertaining to various stages in the discovery process will be examined. Against the two-context theory it will be argued that discovery is a process with an indeterminate number of stages, any of which can be amenable to rational appraisal. The model of discovery as a many faceted process, it will be argued, supersedes the limitations of the two-context theory. Hanson, it would seem, conceded too much to exponents of the two-context theory in that he accepted the distinction between discovery and justification objecting only to the claim that reasoning was not appropriate in the context of discovery. He then attempted to defend a spurious thesis that the mode of reasoning in each context was qualitatively disimilar. Achinstein, who dismisses Hanson's account of two distinct modes of reasoning, nevertheless adheres to the two-context theory, but advances beyond Hanson in his insistence that the mode of reasoning is essentially the same in both contexts. According to Achinstein (1971, p.139) the distinction between the logic of discovery and the logic of justification can be expressed as follows:

If a scientist first came to be acquainted with a hypothesis in the course of reasoning to its truth or plausibility we might say that his reasoning occurred in the context of discovery. If the scientist had been acquainted with the hypothesis before his reasoning occurred and had engaged in the reasoning in the course of attempting to defend the hypothesis we might say that his reasoning took place in the context of justification.

In this respect the distinction between reasons for suggesting H and reasons for accepting H can be maintained if one simply recognises that sometimes one reasons when formulating hypotheses and sometimes one reasons when justifying hypotheses. Achinstein and Hanson are in full agreement against Popper, Reichenbach and Braithwaite, that reasoning occurs in the context of discovery, but they diverge on the issue of whether there is a special mode of reasoning which characterises discovery. Says Achinstein (1971, p.141):

> I agree with Hanson that reasoning takes place when hypotheses are discovered and not only when they are defended. But contrary to what he suggests, the modes of reasoning are the same in both cases. The distinction between discovery and justification, as far as reasoning is concerned, depends not on the model of reasoning but on the state of knowledge of the reasoner and on his purpose, or lack of it, in reasoning.

If Achinstein's thesis is correct, and there is no mode of reasoning specific to the context of discovery, then what is the status of both Peirce and Hanson's appeal to retroductive inference which was held to be a fundamental feature of reasoning in the context of discovery?

Retroduction

Following Peirce, Hanson maintained that it is retroductive inference, rather than deductive or inductive inference, which characterises scientific discovery. Like Peirce, Hanson argued that scientists do not conjecture wildly or blindly in their research, but that the initial conjecture already involves a logical step of discrimination between promising versus implausible categories of hypotheses. The logic of discovery, he held, is the set of inferential steps whereby an anomaly is employed to generate the context in which it is resolved. A scientist begins with a consideration of puzzling phenomena that have been reliably observed. From that an inference is made to a hypothesis. If this turns out to be correct it would explain the phenomena by organising the data into an intelligible, systematic, conceptual pattern. For example, Kepler arrived at his First Law regarding the orbits of the planets neither deductively nor inductively: 'Kepler', says Hanson (1958, a.p.72), 'did not *begin* with the hypothesis that

74

Mars' orbit was elliptical and then deduce statements confirmed by Brahe's observations. These latter observations were given, and they set the problem - they were Johannes Kepler's starting point. He struggled back from these, first to one hypothesis, then to another, then to another, and ultimately to the hypothesis of the elliptical orbit'. Hanson's (1958, b.p.1078) model of retroductive inference can be outlined as follows:

1. Some surprising, astonishing phenomenon P1, P2, P3,... is encountered.
2. But P1, P2, P3,... would not be surprising or astonishing if H were true - they would follow as a matter of course from H; H would therefore explain P1, P2, P3,...
3. Therefore there is good reason for elaborating H - for proposing it as a possible hypothesis from whose assumptions P1, P2, P3,... might be explained.

Kepler's elliptical hypothesis can be represented as follows:

1. The surprising, astonishing discovery that all planetary orbits are elliptical was made by Kepler (1605 to 1619)
2. But such an orbit would not be surprising or astonishing if, in addition to other familiar laws, an inversely varying law of gravitation obtained. Kepler's First Law would follow as a matter of course: indeed the hypothesis could even explain why (since the Sun is part of the foci) the orbits are ellipses in which the planets travel with a non-uniform velocity.
3. Therefore there is good reason for elaborating this hypothesis further, for proposing it as that from which the assumption of which Kepler's First Law might be explained. (ibid, p.1087)

There is another feature of Hanson's retroductive logic, which is often overlooked by commentators: the theory of retroduction is inseparably linked to his doctrine of the theory-loaded character of observations; that scientific observations are mediated through conceptual patterns. Consequently, Hanson's endorsement of a logic of discovery amounts to the claim that we can conclude that some hypotheses are reasonable in certain contexts where what is reasonable is determined by conceptual patterns governing the data. Says Hanson (1958, a.p.90):

Physical theories provide patterns within which data appear intelligible. They constitute a 'conceptual Gestalt'. A

75

theory is not pieced together from observed phenomena; it is rather what makes it possible to observe phenomena as being of a certain sort, and as related to other phenomena. Theories put phenomena into systems. They are built up in 'reverse' - retroductively. A theory is a cluster of conjectures in search of a premise. From the observed properties of phenomena the physicist reasons his way towards a keystone idea from which the properties are explicable as a matter of course.

From these remarks we can see that, for Hanson, theories developed to explain anomalies will therefore be governed by their conceptual organisation, and that any extension of a theory will proceed retroductively in the sense that plausible hypotheses are inferred from the conceptually organised data. Additional hypotheses will have to fit the existing pattern or 'Gestalt'. The scope of additional hypotheses will be restricted to those which offer a plausible explanation of the anomaly. There is, however, another possibility: it might be such that there are no plausible hypotheses which can be incorporated into the pattern and it would then become a matter of determining which aspects of the patterns were of sufficient low epistemic status to become candidates for alteration. As such, it should be recognised that Hanson's model of retroduction as a logic of discovery, is not a method for generating new ideas but a method which indicates which ideas are candidates for further inquiry. This brings us to some of the more penetrating criticisms of Hanson's logic of discovery.

Although his model of retroductive inference, by virtue of its dependence upon the theory of 'pattern recognition', indicates certain restraints upon hypothesis formation, Hanson focuses almost exclusively on the logical form of Peirce's notion of retroductive inference. So much so that Hanson does not develop Peirce's theories concerning the regulative principles which actually underly the choice of explanatory hypotheses. In this respect Hanson does not advance beyond Peirce's appeal to instinct and 'horse sense'.

Furthermore, although Hanson's model tells us how scientists come to prefer one hypothesis over another it does not explain how the hypotheses are actually generated in the first place. Without a logic of generation the H-D exponent can always insist on an irrational element in the initial stages of the discovery. Augustine Brannigan (1981, p.15) has argued that Hanson's logic of discovery ultimately fails to distinguish between discovery and other activities in which knowledge is acquired. He points out that 'by treating the logic of discovery at the outset as a variety of inferential logic conducted by the researcher, Hanson leaves no provision in the analysis for a distinction between discovery and learning'. Consequently, the model does not specify what is special in a logic of discovery. It covers all kinds of learning, from the rat in the maze to the cook whose cakes won't rise. (ibid., p.15)

A further weakness, as Larry Laudan (1980, p.174) has argued, is that whilst abduction may characterise response to an anomaly it cannot provide a rational account of the creative process and is therefore wrongly construed as a logic of discovery: 'abduction', he says, 'does *not* tell us how to invent or discover an hypothesis. It leaves that (possibly creative) process unanalysed and tells us instead where an idea is worthy of pursuit (namely when it explains something we are curious about)'.

But even if all of the above criticisms are valid none undermine the case for a logic of discovery; they may simply indicate where Hanson had failed to provide a satisfactory characterisation of it. Thus Achinstein's criticism of Hanson reveals that discovery is a rational process even though rules cannot be formulated that will guarantee discoveries on every occasion.

Achinstein

Substantial criticism of Hanson's retroductive model has been made by Achinstein, who argues that it grossly under-values the level of background knowledge that is essential for scientific inference. According to Hanson an inference to a law is made from 1) surprising phenomena to 2) the fact that if the law were true, it would explain the phenomena, to 3) the conclusion that there is reason to suggest that the law is true. But as Achinstein (1971, p.118) points out, in many cases scientists do not begin with observed anomalies and furthermore: 'the claim that a scientist always starts by considering simply observed phenomana is unacceptable. Maxwell developed his distribution law for molecular velocities by considering not observed phenomena but the unobserved molecular nature of the gas postulated by the kinetic theory'. In those cases where the reasoning proceeds from an observed anomaly, the theoretical background is one of the more important factors. For a scientist usually knows what he is looking for. Even when a scientist begins with a consideration of observed phenomena this is not all he considers. 'Usually a theoretical background is relevant. Gay-Lussac did not infer his law simply from experiments with hydrogen and oxygen, but from these together with, or in the light of, a theory he held about the molecular structure of gases and forces between molecules'. (ibid, p.118)

We can see here that the alleged weakness of Hanson's account of discovery is his neglect of the theoretical background against which an anomaly is observed. This is the traditional epistemological problem concerning a starting point. Although he recognised that all observations are theory-impregnated, he frequently spoke of beginning with empirical data and then inferring an hypothesis to explain the data. In a very important sense he failed to appreciate the force of his own insight concerning the extent of theory-ladeness in the initial awareness of the problem. In fact problem contexts can be very rich in theoretical content. Yet Hanson's recourse to visual metaphors lend support to a suggestion that problems simply 'pop up' when attention is suddenly directed to 'surprising phenomena'. But as Achinstein demonstrates, this is not how much of research is conducted. A scientist's reasoning to a new hypothesis may not be directed so much by 'surprises' as by certain rational expectations, long term goals, and the needs of everyday routine work. Hanson's emphasis on perceptual analogies unfortunately perpetuated an idea he rejected; that scientific discovery is an event, akin to finding a new species of bug under a rock, rather than as a process of discursive reasoning.

Perhaps the most damaging criticism that Achinstein levels at Hanson is his charge that retroductive inference is ultimately fallacious. According to Achinstein (1971, p.118):

> From the fact that a hypothesis H, if true, would explain the data it does not in general follow that there is reason to think that H is true. The hypothesis that I will be paid $1 million when I complete this book would, if it were true, explain why I am writing the book. But this provides no reason for thinking that I am about to become a millionaire. There are many 'wild' hypotheses which if true would explain the data, but unless there is some other evidence in their favour, this fact by itself lends no plausibility to them.

Unless one appreciates the extent to which the prevailing background knowledge limits the scope of inference, Hanson's retroductive model cannot escape the charge of randomness; the very charge that he levels at the H-D account of discovery.

Achinstein portrays discovery as a rational process and, like Hanson, he maintains that inferences do take place in the context of discovery; that inferences are made to hypotheses. But Achinstein does not see any need to postulate a special kind of reasoning peculiar to discovery. Achinstein (ibid, p.117) outlines three characteristics in an inference. An inference involves 1) 'coming to believe something, that some proposition is true, or probable, or plausible'; 2) 'inferring also involves having a reason for a belief, one's reason being what one infers from it'; and 3) 'the reason must be "evidential", one which the inferrer believes makes it likely that what he infers is true'. Thus: 'To say that a person A inferred p from q is to say 1) that A has come to believe that p is true (or probable, or plausible), and 2) that when A did so his evidential reason for believing this was that q is true'.(ibid, p.118) When drawing an inference one need not be testing an articulated hypotheses or a finished research report. Achinstein (ibid, p.118) employs his model of inference to hypotheses in order to demonstrate how Galileo reasoned in the context of discovery.

> Take Galileo's discovery of mountains and craters on the Moon. With his telescope trained on the Moon, Galileo reported observing several things never before seen. These included numerous small spots all over the lunar surface and the uneven state of the boundary between illuminated and unilluminated parts. He also observed that the small spots have 'blackened parts directed towards the Sun, while on the side opposite the Sun they are crowned with bright colours', and that these spots 'lose their blackness as the illuminated region grows larger and larger'. From these facts and others he made an inference to the hypothesis that 'the surface of the Moon is not smooth, uniform, and precisely spherical as a great number of philosophers believe it (and the other heavenly bodies) to be, but is uneven, rough, and full of cavities and prominences, being not unlike the face of the Earth, relieved by chains of mountains and deep valleys'.

Galileo's inferences to hypotheses in the context of discovery were clearly rational, so were his hypotheses concerning the existence of the moons of Jupiter, which, says Achinstein, were also drawn from observations in the context of discovery. Moreover, as Achinstein points out, the fact that these inferences were rational does not have to indicate the existence of a universal *a priori* rule book whose use will guarantee correct discoveries on every occasion. That is not what a logic of discovery is about. Nevertheless, as Achinstein shows, inferences are made in the context of discovery, and they do not differ substantially from inferences made in the context of justification.

The value of maintaining a two context distinction (since both contexts can be shown to be rational and do not involve distinct kinds of reasoning) will be questioned in the final chapter where a many context approach will be developed. But the importance of Peirce, Hanson, and Achinstein's contribution to arguments concerning the logic of discovery was the legitimacy which they conferred upon philosophical investigations into the discovery process, showing also that discovery is a rational affair. The emphasis of Popper, Reichenbach and Braithwaite, on criteria for the justification of already articulated hypotheses, was bound up with a standpoint which limits philosophical inquiry to a minute realm of scientific practice, ignoring the conceptual and material context in which a hypothesis might be proposed.

If discovery is irrational, if scientists really did suspend reason until after the completion of a research report, and there were no modes of plausible inference in the initial stages of discovery, then no one would have any means of deciding whether a research proposal was worth backing. Yet governments and agencies which decide which research proposal should be supported are not supposed to back wild hunches and potential flights of irrationality. They are supposed to operate with a shrewd idea of what is to be expected. They can, and too often do, finance spectacular failures and ignore potentially fruitful research programmes. Consequently they are rightly criticised for their short-sightedness. Such criticism itself reveals that a relevant criterion for assessing potential discoveries is or ought to be available, even if it has not been adequately applied. The assessment of prototypes has always been part of scientific practice. In certain areas of technology some form of prior assessment is essential; architects who design elevators for high rise flats are legally required to provide guarantees that the end product will function safely, and engineers who design and build faulty bridges may end up in gaol. These guarantees are not all-embracing in the sense that every logically possible contingency can be foreseen and avoided, but they require prior reasoning based on well-established theories and background knowledge. In an important respect the creative scientist, like the engineer, requires a shrewd idea of what will work, what will fit, what will count as a solution to the problem.

The reinstatement of a logic of discovery is not an endorsement of some philosophers stone that will guarantee discovery, but rather a recognition of the need to comprehend the mechanisms which are employed to increase one's chances of making discoveries. Building on the work of Peirce, Hanson and Achinstein what needs to be developed now is an account of the mechanisms by means of which relevant hypotheses are generated and irrelevant ones restricted.

IV Discovery as a mode of problem-solving

Great Moment or Steady Process?

A principal obstacle to a logic of discovery is the fallacious belief that discovery occurs in moments in science of which there can be no logical apparatus for appraisal. This denial of any rational means of theory generation is part of received wisdom in philosophy of science, as the following remarks by Kantorovich and Ne'eman (1989, p.505) indicate:

> It is now widely accepted that there is no logic or universal
> method to arrive at true or successful hypotheses.
> Furthermore, irrespective of the manner in which a given
> theory is discovered, there is no logical or analytic method
> of determining, before testing the theory, whether it is true,
> or what is the probability that it is true. If, indeed, there is
> no rational theory-generating method and no analytic way
> of assessing a theory's validity, there is no *a priori*
> justification for the theory.

Against this view it will be argued here that discovery and creativity are amenable to rational investigation and that they can be analysed as a species of problem solving. Reference will be made to the work of Alan Newell, Herbert A. Simon, Pat. S. Langley, and other early pioneers of

81

Artificial Intelligence research, who argue that some problem solving processes can be simulated by computer programs and are therefore amenable to rational assessment. It will be maintained throughout that there is no qualitative difference between normal problem solving activities and problem solving techniques associated with major turning points in science.

Opponents of a logic of scientific discovery have usually felt on safe ground when they argue against a theory which claims to predict, or give a rational explanation of, great events. But the strength of this objection is only apparent. The reason why a theory of discovery cannot predict great events is that there are no such events. It may be the case that the text-books of science portray discovery this way when they cite Watt's kettle, Fleming's culture, Gray's bath-tub, and Roentgen's X-rays. But these are anecdotal accounts which, in the light of more detailed examination, inevitably turn out to be at best dramatic moments during the course of long and sometimes painful processes requiring thousands of working hours by hundreds of participants. Simon (1977) points out how X-rays were unknown in 1895 but were well-known by 1897; how modern quantum mechanics which did not exist in 1924 clearly did in 1926, but the approach to this knowledge, when looked at closely, was gradual and steady. Kuhn (1970) portrays the Copernican revolution as a dramatic transition akin to a gestalt switch but in his detailed account of its emergence he is fully aware that it took well over a century for completion (Kuhn, 1957). Discovery is not an event, but a process in which many participate over a lengthy period of time. Every major breakthrough is attended by hundreds of industrious scientists. As Simon (1977, p.288) points out: 'This particular slot-machine produces stiff arms for every jackpot'. To explain how Schroedinger and Heisenberg came to quantum mechanics in 1926 it is necessary to explain why Planck, Bohr, Einstein, de Broglie, and many others of similar ability, struggled for over twenty years without completing this discovery. (ibid, p.288)

Is there a significant difference between the conceptual tools required for an explanation of revolutionary discoveries and those required for an explanation of normal routine puzzle-solving science? This question will be addressed in the final section of this chapter. Those who maintain that discovery is a mode of problem solving usually hold the view that there is no significant distinction between routine and revolutionary science. Simon (ibid, p.286) argues that 'all scientific discovery is a form of problem-solving, and that the processes whereby science is carried on can be explained in terms that have been used to explain the processes of problem solving. This thesis also forms the basis of Pat S. Langley, Herbert A. Simon, Gary L. Bradshaw, and Jan M. Zytkow's (1987) investigation into computer simulation of creative discovery processes, where the central hypothesis is 'that the mechanisms of scientific discovery are not peculiar to that activity but can be subsumed as special cases of the general mechanisms of problem solving'. (Langley et al, 1987, p.5) There is, on these terms, nothing further required to explain the mechanisms for solving great problems than the explanations of routine problem solving. But if the great events turn out to be, as Simon argues, lengthy processes of steady application, what is left of the belief in the great minds that are considered pivotal in the development of scientific knowledge? The question can be posed in the following terms:

> Does science depend, for its major progress upon heroes who have faculties not possessed by journeymen scientists? Or are the men whose names we associate with the great discoveries just the lucky one - those who had their hands on the lever at the precise moment when the jackpot showered its rewards? (Simon, 1977, p.288)

Perhaps the jackpot metaphor is unfortunate. It suggests randomness, chance, and luck. There is an element of good fortune in the recognition of major scientific contributions but it is bound up with the social processes which bestow recognition upon a scientist associated with a discovery rather than with the actual discovery itself. There is very frequently a great amount of luck in the discovery process, but it can never outweigh the preparation, anticipation, familiarity with the problem, together with an awareness of the numerous blind alleys - all of which make up the content of the discovering mind. Any discoverer associated with a major development in science is guided in the initial guesswork and essential conclusions by an awareness of the pitfalls encountered by scores of predecessors. Essential to any account of success must be an awareness of the successful person's knowledge of previous failures, for the path to success is regulated by an idea of what would constitute failure. The successful scientist must know how to rule out pre-doomed alternatives. Galileo knew where his predecessors had failed; Newton was aware of the shortcomings of alternative theories of motion, just as Einstein was aware of the mistaken paths that others had taken. When Einstein extended the Principle of Relativity to the whole of physics and in particular to electromagnetism, this was not the outcome of sudden inspiration or an irrational leap. He was aware, at least by the turn of the century, that all attempts at explaining electromagnetic phenomena in mechanistic terms had failed. This meant, for Einstein, that in any choice between either of the two rival theories - Newtonian mechanics and Maxwell's electromagnetic theory - the former would have to give way. As Elie Zahar (1983, p.255) notes: 'Einstein consequently extended the Relativity Principle to the whole of physics, whilst taking Maxwell's equations as his fixed point'. In this way the scope of Einstein's reasoning was necessarily restricted by knowledge of past failure combined with a criterion of what would count as a successful theory - in this instance, a theory that would restore unity to physics.

At any given stage there are the inevitable dead ends and lines of wasteful research. Once committed to a barren research programme not even the greatest mind can score a hit. But, armed with a foreknowledge of the problems together with a knowledge of the erroneous solutions already attempted, there should be nothing remarkable about the attainment of the correct result. This is in line with Simon's (1977, p.288) overall contention that there is 'no evidence that there exists significant differences between the processes that great scientists use in achieving their discoveries and the processes used by those men we merely regard as "good" scientists'. And just as there may not be any significant distinction between the great and the good so there might not be any qualitative differences between 'the *processes* of revolutionary science and normal science, between work of high creativity and journeyman work'. (ibid, p.288) Tales of great scientists and their great discoveries provide less insight into the development of science than they reveal about the interests of historians and their readers. It would be quite dull to read a long record of thousands of minor contributions and unfulfilled research aspirations of minor scientists over a protracted period of time.

One of the most remarkable and creative discoveries in the history of physics is Max Planck's discovery of the Law of Black Body radiation. Yet Langley et al (1987) have demonstrated how the actual derivation by means of which Planck obtained his law in a few hours on October 7th, 1900, involved little more than routine problem solving methods, given his awareness of the problem and the scope of solution space open to him. Having broken down the problems facing Planck into matters of routine research Langley et al conducted a test on eight professional physical scientists (competent in mathematics) who were given the task of solving the crucial interpolation problem without having access to its physical origins. The result was that 'Five gave the same answer that Planck arrived at, each in under two minutes'... although... 'None of them recognised the problem as related to Black Body radiation or thought of Planck's Law until they had derived it'.(ibid, p.53) The authors concluded that, far from being a piece of miraculous insight or irrational intuition, anyone possessing 'the standard heuristics of an applied mathematician (all of which were known

84

in 1900) would not require an extensive search to solve the problem'. (ibid, p.53)

We do not know what went on in Planck's mind at the time, or which of several strategies he might have adopted. But what is clear from Langley et al's example is that 'only standard processes used by and generally available to theoretician's in the physical sciences, need be postulated to explain the actual discovery'. (ibid, p.53)

Scientific discoveries can, on occasions, have a different meaning for philosophers and historians than they do for the scientists engaged in the discovery. What a researcher may experience as routine problem solving may, for a variety of reasons unrelated to the scientist concerned, take on a revolutionary significance. But even when they are aware of the revolutionary potential of their work, scientists on the job are problem solvers, trying to deal with complex problems with the tools at their disposal, reducing complexity to routine. This was as true for Watson and Crick in the 1950's as it is for any journeyman scientist. But historians, biographers, novelists, philosophers, and scientists too, when they reflect on science, may seize on certain episodes to emphasise great dislocations in the history of science.

It is in this context that the phenomenon of reconstitution should be addressed. Scientific practice, not merely the writings of historians of science, transforms and reconstitutes its past so that the very meaning of theories and experiments are constantly subjected to change in status and significance. Changes in background beliefs may significantly transform the status of evidential claims. Brannigan's (1981) account of the reconstitution of the 'Piltdown' discovery (later reconstituted as a fraud, then a hoax) and Sapp's (1990) account of the changing significance of Mendel's research (between the publication of his paper in 1865 and its reconstituted re-emergence in 1901 when applied to a different problem field) are examples of this phenomenon by means of which science itself constantly reconstitutes its past. The Michelson-Morley experiment was once widely believed to have been the source of Einstein's Special Theory of Relativity. The status of this experiment was reconstituted when it was shown that Einstein's work was independent of Michelson and Morley. Lavoisier believed that he had discovered the principle of 'acidity' and the term he introduced, 'oxygen' was taken to mean 'acid producer'. It was later, when Sir Humphrey Davy demonstrated that some acids do not contain oxygen, that Lavoisier's discovery took on a new meaning. Reconstitutions can affect normal as well as revolutionary science, such that transformations in the former may later be given the significance of the latter. An example here is the development of quantum theory during the decades which followed the 'revolution' in quantum theory, which stressed 'profound changes in the way the theory is to be understood and interpreted'.(Bohm and Peat, 1988, pp.83-4) This was clearly a case of problem solving, over time, effecting a reconstitution with revolutionary implications.

The account of scientific discovery as a mode of problem solving, put forward by Simon (1977) and by Langley et al (1987) can be seen as an extension of Pierce and Hanson's attempts to characterise a logic of discovery and is related to recent work in Artificial Intelligence. In this respect Simon (1977, p.289) draws attention to the point that one of the key factors involved in any process of problem solving is that it involves a large amount of 'highly selective trial and error search', using 'rules of thumb' or heuristics as bases for selectivity. Although such rules of thumb are integral to the scientific enterprise they are neither random nor irrational. They are problem-oriented with a background knowledge of unacceptable routes which regulate options. Selective trial and error may take time during which the stock of known unacceptable paths build up and govern the number of future potential paths. It is also important that the criteria for selection are not drawn too widely. In this context Simon cites Jacques Hadamard's (1945, p.48) example of the use of hunting cartidges.

> It is well known that good hunting cartridges are those which have a proper scattering. If this scattering is too wide, it is useless to aim; but if it is too narrow you have too many chances to miss your game by a line.

The appeal here is to trial and error, but it is well-structured trial and error. It resembles what Peirce had in mind when he spoke of 'an aptitude for guessing right'. Factors like luck, persistence, and superior criteria for selection, will nevertheless be important but, as Simon points out, it is probably a combination of all three which is the factor behind some of the major discoveries. Most important are the criteria for selection. The more powerful the heuristic the greater the opportunity to take advantage of luck and for persistence to pay off. It is of no value relying on either luck or persistence alone. One example of persistence is Paul Ehrlich's cure for syphilis which he called 'six-o-six' because it was found on his six hundred and sixth trial. Each of the 605 former attempts 'refuted' his hypothesis concerning the possibility of a chemical cure for syphilis. Ehrlich was not a Popperian and persisted until he eventually succeeded in verifying his hypothesis. But it must be stressed that Ehrlich's belief in a chemical cure for syphilis, although not itself empirically testable, constituted a powerful criterion for selection, ruling out numerous irrelevant solution fields.

It may be the case that when viewed from the top of an ivory tower scientific revolutions are less dramatic. But even among those who have not been blinded by academic detachment the mystery of momentus discoveries begins to evaporate when the numerous short but cumulative steps in a lengthy process of research are examined. Nevertheless, this mystery should not be replaced with an erroneous belief that it is all so simple. As the long and tortuous processes are examined it is then possible to realise how much effort and intelligent application goes into creative work.

Creativity and Computer Simulation of Problem-Solving Processes

In their classic study of creativity Alan Newell, J.C. Shaw, and Herbert A. Simon (Newell et al, 1967) developed a theory of creativity as a form of problem solving, and demonstrated how problem solving computer programs could simulate human problem solving strategies. According to Newell et al, (p.64) a theory of creativity should consist of 1) completely operational specifications for the behaviour of mechanisms (or organisms) that, with appropriate initial conditions, would in fact think creatively; 2) a demonstration that mechanisms which behaved as specified (by these programs) would entail the phenomena that commonly accompanies creative thinking (eg., incubation, illumination, formation and change of set and so forth); 3) a set of statements - verbal or mathematical - about the characteristics of the class of specifications (programs) that includes the particular examples specified. In other words, a theory of creative thought would have to entail the ability to design and build a mechanism that could think creatively and exhibit behaviour akin to a human being carrying out a creative activity. This, as the author's admit, sounds futuristic and utopian. But how utopian is it? A great deal depends on how we interpret the term 'creative'. If we regard all complex problem solving as creative, then it is clear that successful problem solving programs that simulate human problem solvers already exist. But if we reserve the term 'creative' for such things as the discovery of the Special Theory of Relativity or the composition of Beethoven's Seventh Symphony then it is clear that no example of a creative mechanism appears on the horizon. This, however, does not rule out the possibility of ever producing explanatory mechanisms for these creative works; it simply calls for greater awareness of the nature of the problems recognised and tackled by those of the stature of Einstein and Beethoven.

In what sense can existing problem-solving programs be deemed creative? According to Newell et al (ibid, pp.65-6) thinking is creative if one or more of the following conditions are satisfied.

1. The product of the thinking has novelty and value (either for the thinker or the culture).

2. The thinking is unconventional, in the sense that it requires modification or rejection of previously accepted ideas.

3. The thinking requires high motivation and persistence, taking place over a considerable span of time (continuously or intermittently) or at high intensity.

4. The problem as initially posed was vague and ill-defined, so that part of the task was to formulate the problem itself.

Some of the above-mentioned criteria can be found in any of the major creative developments in both the sciences and the arts. But the same features are characteristic of routine problem solving. Leaving aside factors bound up with socio-economic or political interests, such as the recognition which posterity bestows upon the creative work of some individuals, and the greatness often attached to those who allegedly arrived first at an idea or conclusion, the essential features of creative work can be found in either routine problem solving or work associated with revolutionary significance.

The belief that all forms of creative thinking are essentially modes of problem solving is one of the cornerstones of the discipline which has been unfortunately described as 'Artificial Intelligence'. Although Artificial Intelligence has recently become fashionable, with governments and their military connections, industry and finance, expecting miraculous results, research in this area has been going on since the early 1950's. The origins of Artificial Intelligence as a serious discipline can be traced back to the summer of 1956, when a group of investigators met at Dartmouth College to discuss the possibility of constructing genuinely intelligent machines. Among those concerned were Arthur L. Samuel of the International Business Machine Corporation, who had already written a program that played a good game of checkers, and Alan Newell, J.C. Shaw and Herbert A. Simon of the Rand Corporation, who had constructed a logic theorem solving program which was capable of discovering proofs for theorems in elementary symbolic logic using heuristic techniques similar to those employed by humans. (Newell et al, 1967) At that time Newell and Simon were working on a program known as a 'General Problem Solver' which administered a hierarchy of goal-seeking sub-programs. After the Dartmouth Conference, Newell and Simon built up a research group at the

Carnegie Institute of Technology with the goal of developing models of human behaviour, particularly in its creative aspect.

Research workers in Artificial Intelligence maintain that the processes with which human beings successfully solve problems can, in principle, be simulated by computer programs. It is unfortunate that they have exposed themselves needlessly to philosophical criticism concerning the extent to which computers can or cannot simulate the mental apparatus of human beings. To avoid this criticism it is worth emphasising that research on artificially intelligent problem-solvers need not be linked to theories of human intelligence, still less as a contribution to the philosophy of mind. It is simply about the rational conditions for solving problems. A logic of discovery, in this respect, is not a theory of human intelligence. The question facing those who defend a logic of discovery is simply that of giving a rational account of the processes by means of which problems are either solved or transformed. The status of a logic of discovery need not be affected by questions of whether computers can make discoveries initiating periods of revolutionary science, or even whether they can make discoveries at all. Although if a computer could make a discovery in normal science, it should be capable, on the basis of arguments advanced here, of making revolutionary discoveries, as there is no qualitative distinction between these two types of discovery processes.

It is worth mentioning that the attempt to simulate human problem solving has proved harder than first thought. In 1981 the Japanese Ministry of International Trade and Industry confidently predicted that Japan would build a fifth generation computer within ten years, and from then onwards provided large scale financial backing (in the region of 200 million between 1981 and 1989) to the production of a prototype computer based on parallel processes and capable of human-like reasoning. But whilst successes were achieved with regard to information storage, in the amount of electronics packed into a microchip, there has been little achievement in simulating the most elementary forms of cognition akin to seeing and feeling. Moreover, there is good reason to suspect that parallel processing does not simulate human creativity, which seems to rely heavily on images, pattern recognition and sequential reasoning. The foremost critics of claims made on behalf of computer creativity are Weizenbaum (1984) and Dreyfus (1972). However, significant advances have been made which include the WISARD pattern recognition machine at Brunel University, England, which receives information from an optical scanner. When it is presented with an unfamiliar pattern it employs a system of parallel processors to compare it with patterns which are familiar to it. The extent to which this matches human pattern recognition techniques is in its ability to assign a weighting to, or choose, the nearest pattern rather than exhaustively search through every combination for an identical match.

Computer simulation of problem solving may be a useful prototype for the rational assessment of discovery processes, which is why it will be considered here, but the status of a logic of discovery need not stand or fall with the fortunes of computer science. Some of the theories of the Artificial Intelligentsia, it will be argued, are helpful in formulating a rational account of the discovery process. But this inquiry is not limited to the formal mechanisms of computer simulation. Even if it were widely demonstrated that computers cannot, and never could, make discoveries, the case for a logic of discovery could still be maintained.

Chess playing programs have been proposed as simulations of human problem solving processes. Some of them have been in existence for over thirty years. Other early attempts to simulate problem solving processes included musical composition, using Palestrina's rules of counterpoint. (Newell et al, 1967) Several programs were aimed at decreasing the difference between the present intermediate stage and the final goal. The General Problem Solver employed a 'means-end analysis', which compared the present step and the final goal and then decided what to do in order to decrease the difference. Critics have since pointed out that this program was 'a very slow processor of problems'. (Watanabe, 1985, p.133) Other critics have argued that it represented an all too simplistic notion of problem solving. (Weizenbaum, 1984, pp.202-3) Computer programs have long been written for the design of various mechanical appliances. According to Newell et al (1967, p.68): 'These programs take as their inputs the customer's design specifications and produce as their outputs the manufacturing specifications that are sent to the factory floor. They do not make calculations needed in the design process, but actually carry out the analysis itself and make decisions that were formerly the province of the design engineers'.

These processes of discovering proofs for mathematical theorems, composing music, playing chess, and designing engineering structures, would all be considered creative if the product had novelty and originality, and was of a high quality. But even if these problem-solving programs are mundane, they are still modes of creativity. Novelty and originality are not the essential features of a creative problem solving process; they are characteristics associated with being first. If imitiation and plagiarism are excluded the problem solving processes may be independently identical for more than one problem solver. Priority and novelty provide criteria for recognition which are cultural features bound up with esteem and financial reward; they do not characterise the problem solving process itself. The Logic Theorist program, devised by Newell et al, proved capable of reinventing Chapter Two of Russell and Whitehead's *Principia Mathematica*, rediscovering in many cases the same proofs that Russell and Whitehead had done originally. But the Logic Theorist program did not receive any aclaim for its discoveries; this was not because it was lacking in creativity, but rather because Russell and Whitehead had done it first. Nevertheless, just as later generations of scientists improve on earlier formulations without receiving the aclaim bestowed upon the originators, so the Logic Theorist discovered a proof for a theorem in Chapter Two of *Principia Mathematica* that was far shorter and more elegant than the one published by Russell and Whitehead. (Newell et al, 1967)

Many of the more recent discovery programs have proven successful in rediscovering major scientific theories, although it must be acknowledged that their first objective is not to reproduce the historic details of these discoveries but to function as models of how discoveries might occur in various problem fields.

Some of the most successful discovery programs have been concerned with mathematical problem solving. D.B. Lenat's (1977) AM program has rediscovered concepts in number theory. Its criterion for success is not merely that a concept is compatible with empirical data, but 'interesting' in its relationship with other concepts. This program has about 100 basic mathematical concepts such as sets, lists, equality, and operation, and about 250 heuristics to direct the discovery process. New tests are ordered in terms of their 'interestingness'. So far AM's search through mathematical concepts has produced definitions for 'the integers, for multiplication, for division of, and for prime numbers, and proposed the unique-factorization theorem'. (Langley et al, 1987, p.61)

One of the most outstanding discovery programs is the BACON program devised by Langley, Simon, Bradshaw, and Zytkow. BACON is actually a series of programs of increasing refinement, which can be described as a sequence of Artificial Intelligence systems concerned with the discovery of empirical laws. Using data of the kind available to Galileo, Kepler, Boyle, George Simon Ohm, and Coloumb, it has rediscovered Galileo's Law of Uniform Acceleration, Kepler's 3rd Law, Boyle's Law, Ohm's Law, and Coloumb's Law. It has also rediscovered Archimedes' Law of Displacement, Snell's Law of Refraction, and Black's Law of Specific Heat.

The first system, BACON 1, was a data driven program which was limited to giving summaries of the data it 'observed'. But it could not advance beyond these summaries by treating them as data. Later programs achieved greater simulation of the approaches taken by working scientists, such that the BACON 3 program was designed to operate in experimental domains. It overcame BACON 1's distinction between data and laws by allowing different levels of description, and it proceeds, like a working scientist, by means of a 'search through two distinct problem spaces: the space of data and the space of laws'. (Langley et al, 1987, p.88) The advantage of BACON 3 lies in its ability to represent information at multiple levels of description and also in its ability to redefine 'its problem space in the light of previous experience, so that considerable less research is required'. (ibid, p.92)

Among the rediscoveries of BACON 3 and 4 are Ohm's Law, which is inferred from data on the varieties of electrical current with the lengths of the resistance wire in a circuit, and Kepler's 3rd Law, which states that the periods of the planets about the Sun are as the 3/2 power of their distances from the Sun. In fact BACON 3 actually arrived at a more complex version of Kepler's 3rd Law which also subsumed a simplified version of the 2nd Law (that the lines joining a planet with the Sun sweeps out equal areas in equal times) as well. (Schaffner, 1985, p.6)

It is not claimed that BACON's discoveries necessarily followed the same process as those originally associated with them. For example, BACON 3 arrived at Coloumb's Law of 1785 'by means of data-driven induction not influenced by any theory. In contrast, Coloumb was prepared for the appearance of an inverse-square law by the analogies of electrical and magnetic forces to Newtonian gravitational force. Thus whereas Coloumb needed only to test the hypothesis suggested by the analogy, BACON has to discover the law by searching through the space of functions'. (Langley et al, 1987, p.103) In this respect BACON falls short of a complete simulation of Coloumb's method, but nevertheless reveals that the process can be simulated.

BACON 3 has limitations which have been addressed in later programs. It is restricted to the discovery of quantitative empirical laws, and whilst such laws are found in physics, other branches of science involve more qualitative relations. A more sophisticated BACON 4 program employs what are known as 'intrinsic property' heuristics to arrive at several laws in the history of science, such as Archimedes' Law of Displacement, and its development of the concepts of volume and density; Snell's Law of Refraction, and Black's Law of Specific Heat. BACON 4 is an even more sophisticated attempt to simulate methods used by actual researchers. Its key notions are those of 'nominal variables' and 'intrinsic properties': two notions which facilitate a 'move beyond simple summaries of the data to the beginnings of explanation'. (ibid, p.169) Even greater sophistication is achieved by BACON 5 which employs forms of analogical reasoning and has discovered, by a slightly different route, several conservation laws. By using an assumption of symmetry BACON 5 is more theory driven than its predecessors. But whereas the BACON programs exhibit quantitative laws, a more sophisticated program, GLAUBER, rediscovers qualitative laws of the kind discovered by seventeen century chemists, such as the development of the theory of acids and bases. To this end GLAUBER relies upon values for reactions and tastes, such as salty and bitter. (ibid, p.221)

There are certain advantages which successive generations of problem solvers have over their predecessors; they have access to techniques and theories which were not available to the originators, and may even have been derived in various ways from the original product. And, unlike Russell and Whitehead, successive problem solvers, like the Logic Theorist and Lenat's AM program, do not have to discover the problems. Nevertheless, a lack of originality in this domain does not, in itself, demonstrate any significant distinction between the respective modes of reasoning employed by the scientists and the programs which simulate their achievements. Problem articulation is, however, a very important aspect of creative problem solving, which is why Newell et al drew attention to it in their requirements for a theory of creativity. In a limited sense the Logic Theorist did prove capable of selecting problems. 'In working backwards from the goal of proving one theorem, it can conjecture new theories - or supposed theorems - and set up the subgoal of proving these. (Newell et al, 1967, p.70) This, it is claimed, is exactly the same process by which Whitehead and Russell generated the theorems they undertook to prove. For the task they undertook was to derive the basic postulates of arithmetic from the axioms of logic.

There may be many fundamental differences between the Logic Theorist and Russell and Whitehead, as there are between the BACON program and the theories associated with Galileo, Kepler, Boyle, Ohm, Coloumb, Snell and Black. But what is of lasting importance in the research undertaken by Newell et al, is that the boundary between the two modes of problem solving is not as obvious as it is commonly thought.

Solution Generators

Any understanding of the nature of problem solving processes must take into consideration the interplay between solution generating processes and solution restricting processes. This important point was stressed by Newell et al (1967, p.72) when they drew attention to a distinction between processes for 'finding possible solutions' and processes for 'determining whether a solution proposal is in fact a solution'. This should not be seen as a return to the distinction between the context of discovery and the context of justification, as exponents of the two-context distinction insist that rational processes do not occur in the former context. According to the distinction proposed by Newell et al, both sets of processes are amenable to rational assessment.

Solution generating processes may range from methods which involve brute force, triggering mechanisms, blanket trial and error search, to 'extensive calculators that select an appropriate solution at the first try or to elaborate analytic processes that construct a solution of some kind of "working backwards" from the known properties of solutions'. (ibid, p.72) On the other hand solution restrictors are the guiding principles and devices which limit hypotheses. In many popular accounts of discovery the objective is that of finding ways of generating solutions and rich hypotheses. But in reality the successful method involves a combination of both processes of generating hypotheses with the systematic exclusion of wilder and implausible hypotheses.

One well known method of generating solutions is by means of brute force. A small quantity of high explosives may remove a blockage that would take many hours of physical effort to remove. But brute force has obvious limitations, especially in a delicate environment. Nevertheless, a brute force search, which considers every possibility, regardless of its likelyhood, through a finite problem space, will inevitably come up with a solution which may have been hidden in that space. This, it must be stressed, depends on some prior awareness that the solution would be recognised as a solution. If a murder weapon is known to have been hidden in a wood and a sufficient number of police literally comb the entire area for long enough they will inevitably find it. If a criminal is known to be in a certain area and if the police investigate every member of the community, regarding each one with with equal suspicion, checking out every alibi, then such a brute force search (despite many false leads) just might pay off.

The use of computers in searches through a problem space can give the method of brute force greater appeal by virtue of the computer's speed, especially if it is capable of parallel searches. It might be said that human superiority over computers in problem solving is partly due to the structures more amenable to brute force search, such as the built-in parallel processing structures of the human eye and ear. But in practice few human problem solvers employ strict brute force methods preferring, as Peirce noted, some form of prior-assessment. Brute force, then, involves an exhaustive search of all possibilities regardless of their likelihood. As such the advantages of brute force solution generators may be relative to the size of the computer, its memory, speed in manipulation of symbols, in the search among possible solutions.

Brute force methods must be distinguished from algorithmic procedures. An algorithm, whether brutish or not, is a procedure which guarantees a solution. In an attempt to discover the solution to a crossword

94

puzzle an algorithmic search might cover every plausible alphabetical combination to find the missing three letters of a word. This need not be an instance of brute force, as combinations like ZXQ, which do not feature in any English word, need not be applied. Perhaps the most famous example of an algorithmic search is what Simon (1977) refers to as the British Museum algorithm, so named after the monkeys who will sit there patiently attempting to type out the complete works of Shakespeare by randomly hitting keys on a number of typewriters. Eventually they might manage a couple of sonnets but it would be unadvisable to wait for them. Yet, given time and a sufficient stock of typewriters, the task could be completed. The problem with this algorithm becomes obvious once we consider the amount of time required to exhaust all possibilities. After making reasonable assumptions concerning typing speed, the mathematician, Frank W. Cousins, estimated that the chance of an occasional *Hamlet* appearing would occur every $10^{460,000}$ seconds. Michael Crowe (1988, p.553) illustrates this graphically: 'imagine a universe containing a billion galaxies, each made up of a billion stars, around each of which a hundred planets revolve. Place a billion monkeys on each of these planets and set them typing for fifteen billion years (the approximate age of the universe). This would produce only 10^{46} seconds of typing time towards the $10^{460,000}$ seconds needed.

Another popular algorithm is the 'travelling salesman problem', which actually has practical implications (for example, the possible siting of a central power station for an interconnecting grid). Given the geographical location of, say fifty cities, the problem is that of finding the routing that will take the salesman to all the cities with the shortage mileage. The problem here is the straightforward optimising algorithm: try all possible routes and pick the shortest. Yet this algorithm is computationally unfeasable and belongs with the British Museum algorithm.

Many problems can be solved, in principle, by tracing out every possibility. In chess, it would seem feasible, given time, to trace out all possible moves, all of one's opponents possible replies, and so on, as the number of moves is technically finite. If this could be done a player could then decide which move had the best chance of leading to victory. But in practice this is impossible, even for the fastest computers. A chess player would have to consider 10^{120} different board positions in tracking down every possible line of play. Or as John Haugeland (1987, p.16) points out: if we assume an average of 31.6 options per play then 'looking ahead five moves could involve a quadrillion (10^{15}) possibilities; forty moves (a typical game) would involve 10^{20}'. Imagine how long this would take if it only took a fraction of a second to consider each move. For the estimated age of our planetary system is only 10^{18} seconds.

These numbers are too large for any sensible computer and the problems associated with them have been described by the mathematician, Sir James Lighthill, as a 'combinatorial explosion'. One of the problems with the chess playing programs of the 1960's, and the early programs for proving mathematical theorems, was that these schemes were too often 'swallowed up by the exponential expansion of the problem space with deeper and deeper search'. (Simon, 1985, p.74) But human chess players do not perform in this way. They consider only a few possibilities and discard the rest, because many possibilities are obviously stupid. Another important distinction between human chess players and brute force algorithms is that humans do not employ the rules of chess as axioms from which they can generate all possible games. Instead of a brutish search which scans every possible game grandmasters usually operate with remembered patterns which function as heuristic restraints on improbable moves. For this reason computer simulation of human pattern-recognition processes, such as WISARD, do not rely on algorithmic procedures, but simply settle for the most satisfactory likeness in terms of the highest score or the degree of match. Nevertheless, computer speed need not be discounted, for it may have an advantage in some contexts. In a chess search restricted to three possibilities, looking ahead to five moves on either side would involve an investigation of 59,049 combinations, which is still beyond the range of the human mind but within the scope of a computer. But the problem raised by Haugeland (1987, pp.16-17) might still remain, for he objects that 'there is no fail-safe way to tell what is and what is'nt relevant. Everybody knows how a seemingly pointless or terrible move can turn out to be a brilliant stroke (once the opponent takes the bait)'.

In reply to Haugeland's objection it might be said that too much is being asked of the computer. No one expects of a grandmaster that every move in every game is based on guidelines which guarantee success on every occasion. Fortunately, more recent chess playing programs no longer have to rely on brute force or algorithmic methods but are assisted with rules or directions for thinking which reduce the scope of the search. Chess playing programs can now employ evaluatory functions which contain knowledge about which moves are likely to enhance king safety, control of the centre of the board, and so on. They may be programmed to 'size up' a situation, choose the most plausible moves, using information gained in previous attempts to steer subsequent analysis in better directions. Some of these chess playing programs are very good. One program - the Greenblatt Chess Program - wins 80% of its games against non-tournament players and a respectable number against tournament players. It achieved recognition in the form of a honorary membership of the US Chess

Federation. At present the most advanced chess playing system is Deep Thought, which is capable of generating 720,000 moves each second. It was beaten in 1989 by the world chess champion, Gary Kasparov, who claimed that he was playing for the human race. (*The Guardian*, 24 November, 1989)

Solution Restrictors

In many problem solving contexts the question is not how to generate the maximum number of solutions, but how to select the most plausible. According to Jack Myers, (1985) a leading authority in internal medicine, the working memory of a clinician can hold only about five hypotheses at any given time. Only the more brilliant ever exceed that number. The maximum known is seven. It is therefore important that some criterion is operative for the selection of the better hypotheses for consideration. What applies to the clinician in this respect applies equally to the scientist and inventor.

Perhaps the most salvagable aspect of theories of abductive inference is the account of hypothesis regulation in the initial phase of discovery. Gary Gutting (1980, p.226) drew attention to this neglected aspect of Peirce's version of abductive inference, namely: 'its dependence on a set of principles regulating the choice of the explanatory hypothesis'. According to Gutting it is 'those regulative principles of abduction' that illustrate the logic of invention, for they mark out the condition and appropriateness for answering a specific scientific question. Regulative principles can be classified into three types.

1. Principles based on efficiency, which are not concerned directly with the intrinsic merits of a hypothesis but are concerned with limiting their number.

2. Overall scientific intentions or goals, which would include general objectives such as truth-seeking, explanation, prediction, control, or problem-solving.

3. Metaphysical principles concerning the nature of the world of the kind that influenced the ideas of Newton, Bohr, and Einstein.

More specifically, a scientist's background knowledge inevitably functions as a solution restrictor. Wesley C. Salmon (1970) suggests three candidates as instantly implausible ideas: 1) Velikovsky's hypothesis about the origins of Venus; 2) any E.S.P. theory that postulates a transfer of information at a speed faster than light; 3) any teleological biological theory. 'They strike me as implausible', says Salmon (1970, p.80), 'because in one way or another they do not fit well with currently adopted scientific theory'. To an experienced scientist the problems addressed by these theories are spurious and the solutions irrelevant. But to an audience unfamiliar with established scientific knowledge the degree of their incompatibility with other long adopted theories might not be noticed, and their instant dismissal could be seen as professional narrow-mindedness. Yet despite those oft-cited examples where the tables have been turned on blinkered professionals the adoption of an entirely open-mind policy would not enhance creativity; it would simply replace selective constraint with brute force trial and error search.

In many fields of invention and discovery a working knowledge of scientific laws will block off pre-doomed hypotheses. The knowledge of the principles governing energy, formulated in the 1830's, not only enhanced scientific and technical developments, it also eliminated - for those who understood them - many attempts to manufacture perpetual motion machines. Knowledge of scientific laws can place initial restraints on imaginative fiction. A background knowledge of the problem of scaling would certainly eliminate many pre-doomed investigative paths. Contrary to the beliefs of many science-fiction readers large scale replicas cannot function if reproduced in exact proportion to small scale originals. For example, it is often said that given an ant's ability to lift many times its own weight, were the ant scaled up to the size of an elephant its physical strength would be beyond anything imaginable. However, an understanding of scaling will soon eliminate such science-fiction nightmares - along with optimistic beliefs in genetically programmed chickens the size of cattle. Since Galileo physicists, designers and architects, have been aware of the problem of scaling. Galileo noted, with regard to structures having the same physical characteristics, such as shape, density, or chemical composition, that weight W increases linearly with volume V, whereas strength only increases like a cross sectional area A. Given similar structures $V \alpha L^3$ and $A \alpha L^2$, where L is a characteristic length or height, it can be concluded that

$$\frac{\underline{Strength}}{Weight} \quad \alpha \quad \frac{A}{V} \quad \alpha \quad \frac{1}{L} \quad \propto \quad \frac{1}{W^1/3}$$

Although smaller animals may appear stronger than larger ones, and ants appear - relatively speaking - stronger than elephants, their advantage would not survive scaling. If an ant were scaled up to the size of an elephant its weight would increase faster than its strength, ultimately causing it to collapse under its own weight. Thus the fantasies of science-fiction writers of giant ants, spiders and the like, can never be realized. The giant worms in *Dune* are physically as well as biologically impossible. For similar reasons humans cannot fly under their own muscle power, whilst small animals can leap proportionately greater distances than larger ones. These principles are recognised and applied by architects, designers, ship-builders and biologists, and have also played a profound regulatory role in hypothesis generation in subject areas as diverse as engineering, aeronautics, quantum field theory, sub-atomic and high energy physics. (West, 1988, pp.2-21)

When philosophers speak of regulative background knowledge they usually think of ideas or theories. But as Ronald N. Giere shows, much of the background knowledge is in the form of embodied knowledge in the technology used in performing experiments. The very design of equipment used by scientists embodies regulative background knowledge. 'The cyclotron', says Giere (1988, p.140), 'was designed with the intention of using it to accelerate protons, among other things. The design may therefore be thought of as embodying some of our knowledge about photons, such as their charge and mass'. When the first cyclotrons were built in the 1930's no one thought of producing spin-polarized protons. Now, says Giere (ibid, p.140), 'the knowledge of how to produce these beams is part of embodied knowledge in the design of modern cyclotrons'.

Apart from the regulative force of background knowledge are various preferences held by scientists over the kind of explanations they would accept. When seeking alternative explanations to existing ones scientists frequently place constraints on the kind of explanations they will consider. Einstein insisted on economy, simplicity and internal consistency, as restraining conditions. As Richard Scheines (1987, p.363) points out, in 1905 Einstein revealed a 'flaw in the way traditional electrodynamics explained the phenomenon of inducing a current in a coil with a magnet. He pointed out that the two situations - the coil still and the magnet moving, and the coil moving and the magnet still - were perfectly symmetrical physically, yet the theoretical explanations of them are asymmetric'. 'In effect', says Scheines (ibid, p.363): 'Einstein invoked a principle of explanatory adequacy to argue that the traditional theory needed to be changed, and then a principle of relative explanatory virtue to argue for the theoretical apparatus he introduced as an alternative to Maxwell's and Lorentz's theory. Einstein placed constraints on the type of explanations he was searching for. They had to have certain symmetry properties, they had to be simple, and of course they had to account for a wide range of already established empirical phenomena'.

It should also be noted that the principles of hypothesis restraint, employed by Einstein and many others, also served as criteria for theory adoption - an issue which will be examined later. It would appear that for Einstein there was no significant distinction between the reasoning processes which produced his initial hypotheses and the processes by means of which he put them forward as adopted explanations.

Apart from regulative principles for hypothesis restraint other methods of combatting a potential explosion of search space may involve the use of techniques of selectivity. Rules might be introduced for searching only part of the space without actually missing the solution, or one might adopt strategies which eschew absolute guarantees of reaching an exact solution, resorting instead to various rules of thumb that indicate more promising regions of the search space. In chess, for example, it is hardly constructive to search through every possible move. As Simon (1985, p.74) points out: 'A good example is the use of expert chess knowledge to incorporate a plausible move generator in a chess program, so that not all moves will have to be examined but only those that give promise of being good moves'.

Given the advantage of computer speed over much slower human thought processes it would seem that the way forward is by means of a combination of speed of search with regulatory rules. In this context Simon speaks of a dialectic between machine power and criteria for selectivity, with no clear verdict in favour of either approach. Thus some of the current chess programs contain considerable background knowledge concerning successful strategies which do not require an exhaustive search. But as the potential for computers to achieve new levels of speed and memory capacity increases, the balance moves back in favour of brute force again. Some programs for master chess now examine several million possibilities before selecting a move - and do so in a matter of minutes. The computer team who devised Deep Thought are said to be working on a program that will, by 1992, think through a billion moves each second. Combine this speed with a background knowledge of chess, regulatory principles, and an evaluatory function, and we have an Hegelian synthesis between brute force and intelligent selection.

One elementary example of tempering brute force with solution restraint is Newell et al's (1967) account of an enterprising thief attempting to find the correct combination of numbers to open a safe. It will soon become apparent that without knowledge of the combination one either requires a lot of patience and time if a brute force search is employed or some kind of technique for reducing the size of the search space. Newell et al (ibid, p.77) describe the safe-cracker problem as follows:

Consider a safe whose lock has ten independent dials, each with numbers running from 00 to 99 on its face. The safe will have $100^{10} = 10^{20}$, or one hundred billion billion possible settings, only one of which will unlock it. A would-be-safe cracker, twirling the dials at random, would take on average fifty billion billion trials to open it.

However, if the safe were defective, so that there was a faint click each time any dial was turned to its correct setting, it would take an average of only fifty trials to find the correct setting of any one dial, or five hundred trials to open the safe. The ten successive clicks that told him when he was getting 'warmer' would make all the difference to the person opening the safe between an impossible task and a trivial one.

There are no absolutely fail-safe guidelines for solving problems, but methods of solution restriction can be taught in class rooms, such as the tried and tested techniques of reducing complex problems to simple problems. In his *Rules for the Conduct of the Understanding*, Descartes advised would-be problem solvers to 'reduce involved and obscure propositions step by step to those that are simpler, and then starting with the intuitive apprehension of all those that are absolutely simple, attempt to ascend the knowledge of all the others by precisely similar steps'. (Descartes, 1911, 14) One method he would have endorsed is the reduction of complex problems by a three step process. First, break down the problem into sub-problems, keeping a record of the relations between these parts as part of the total problem. Second, solve the sub-problems. Third, combine the results to form a solution to the problem as a whole. If the sub-problem is too complex, repeat the procedure again. When breaking down problems into sub- problems, the key to success lies in the initial description of the problem. A correct identification and description of the problem invariably contains the analogies and metaphors which can generate and regulate plausible solutions.

Problem solving, we have argued, does not depend primarily upon solution-generation; there have to be mechanisms which restrict the number of solutions suggested by the given data. Science is not merely about gaining knowledge; it is also concerned with the way knowledge is gained. This simple point is often neglected by exponents of the 'generate and test' approach where anything goes in the generative stage. Moreover, the requirement for restriction is not merely to reduce pointless inductive generalisations, but also pointless deductive ones too, which suggests that the inductive- deductive distinction - at least with respect to solution restraint - is not as important as it might otherwise seem. For example, we can infer the mortality of Socrates from his masculinity deductively. This might be important as well as valid. But valid deductive inferences such as the inference from the knowledge that the chalk is white to 'either chalk is white or pigs can fly' are as worthless as they are valid. The relevance of any inference in the discovery process must be bound up with the current knowledge within the system in question.

That working scientists operate with criteria for hypothesis restriction rather than brute force search was fundamental to Peirce's account of discovery. For Peirce (1931-58, 5.p.172), brute force was clearly an irrational technique.

> A physicist comes across some new phenomenon in his laboratory. How does he know that the conjunctions of the planets have something to do with it or that it is not perhaps that the dowager empress of China has at that time a year ago chanced to pronounce some word of mystical power or that some invisible jinnee may be present. Think of what trillions and trillions of hypotheses might be made of which one only is true; and yet after two or three, or at the very most a dozen guesses, the physicist hits pretty nearly on the correct hypothesis. By chance he would not have been likely to do in the whole time that has elapsed since the earth was solidified.

Heuristics

Methods of eliminating unfavourable solutions, narrowing down the search space, breaking complex problems into sub-problems, are essential features of both human and computer-based problem solving techniques. Following George Polya (1957) the term 'heuristics' has been given to methods of problem solving which seek to direct the search. Heuristics comes from the Greek word for 'discover' which is contrasted with 'algorithm' from the Latin word for the Arabic system of numbers, so named after the Arab mathematician. The notion of a 'heuristic search' has served as a foundation stone for later work in Artificial Intelligence research. According to Newell et al (1967, p.78) the term 'heuristic' denotes 'any principle or device that contributes to the reduction in the average search to a solution'. Heuristics are directions for thinking - usually, but not always, in terms of reducing the scope of the search - and although they may be algorithmic, they may be, and usually are, employed as useful rules of thumb for directed search. Heuristic 'rules of thumb' are not sub-standard pieces of equipment, as some detractors suggest, because they can be assessed, improved, or replaced with superior rules. Heuristic directed programs differ from algorithmic searches with respect to the kind of guarantee they impart to their conclusions. Heuristic directed programs offer solutions but do not guarantee them in a way that an algorithm would. However, given the fact that brute force random searches are frequently irrational, and that some algorithms require millenia, then heuristic searches are convenient and practically important forms of solution restriction.

The process of searching for 'good enough' rules of thumb is called 'satisficing'. (Simon, 1977, p.173) Heuristics may be deemed 'good enough' but if they are not then others are found. Simon's example of selling a house is a helpful illustration. A vendor may have no definite idea of the house's value, but makes an estimate, based on an appraisal of the cost of similar property in the area (background knowledge). If the bids come in near this figure, he holds to it. If they do not he gradually reduces it. When a bid comes near to the revised figure he accepts it. This is called 'satisficing'. It is a rational way of selling a house. The criterion of 'good enough' is called an 'aspiration level'. A rational method of selling a house, such as this, should not be tied to any dogmatic insistence on a guaranteed sale price for every house. Both the goal and the criterion for 'good enough' are subject to revision, and both can be subjected to appraisal and assessment.

Practical researchers would find it more relevant if philosophers investigated criteria for the assessment of satisficing conditions, rather than search for foundational certitude. One promising avenue in this direction is Ronald N. Giere's (1988) assessment of satisficing criteria for the adoption of scientific models in nuclear physics and also in the 'plate techtonics' revolution in the earth sciences. In both of these case studies Giere shows how scientists do not reason axiomatically from foundational theories, but select models according to satisficing criteria. A similar approach can be attributed to Kepler's discovery of the elliptical orbits of the planets, which was based on observations which met satisficing criteria rather than certitude. Using Tycho Brahe's observations, Kepler, after making numerous calculations, eventually arrived at the hypothesis that the orbit of Mars was elliptical and likewise for the other planets. But in fact these orbits were not perfect ellipses because, as Newton later demonstrated, each planet is affected by the mass of other planets as well as by the Sun. But Tycho Brahe's observations, although strictly speaking inaccurate, were satisfactory enough for Kepler to propose elliptical orbits, and the inaccuracy was too small for Kepler to detect any discrepancy. For the job in hand Brahe's calculations were 'good enough'.

One of the main objections to accounts of heuristic directed searches is similar to the objections to the possibility of providing a logical account of discovery. It is therefore appropriate to consider the objection here. Briefly stated the objection concerns the epistemological status of a heuristic search; there are no guarantees that it can deliver the truth. This objection deserves to be tackled head on. It is necessary to ask what value could there possibly be in a methodology which demands one hundred per cent certainty as a precondition for any kind of research? The demand for a methodology which requires absolute maximisation of truth content has its origins in Cartesian-Humean skepticism, which might be invoked to sharpen the wits of philosophy students, but has no relevance to the practice and understanding of scientific inquiry. As Thomas Nickles (1987, p.125) points out: 'every methodology which has taken Hume's problem of induction too seriously has impoverished itself to the point of infertility'. Fortunately, practical engineers, designers, architects, and the majority of scientific researchers, cannot afford the luxury of taking Descartes and Hume's problems too seriously.

Contrary to popular views truth is neither the sole nor the primary objective of science or scientific methodology. The truth can be trivial and inappropriate, as Nelson Goodman and Catherine Z. Elgin (1988, p.52) indicate: 'Having been ordered to shoot anyone who moved the guard shot all the prisoners, contending that they were all moving rapidly around the Sun. Although true, his contention was plainly wrong, for it involved an inappropriate category of motion'. Truth-seeking is a scientific virtue in the same way that dishonest research is worthless, but a methodology geared to truth-maximisation can be destructive to that end, especially when applied to an embryonic research program.

Although it is generally advisable to test a theory wherever possible, and testing is linked to verisimilitude, it is not unscientific to adopt without a test. Scientists just have to adopt theories without detailed tests. They only have a few decades, at most, in which to add to the stock of scientific knowledge. This necessitates that many short cuts have to be taken, that many theories have to be taken for granted. This naturally adds to the risk that many adopted theories will be mistaken. But even the most direct knowledge claims are fallible. On these terms science is best served by severing it from all claims to absolute certitude, and from all methodologies designed to promote them.

Against the Cartesian-Humean inspired demand for a methodology linked to absolute truth is the Peircian maxim 'Do not block off the road to inquiry', which Nickles (1987) cites along with Simon's account of 'bounded rationality', according to which a researcher should seek 'satisficing conditions' for the most efficient method of problem solving.

It is inherently counter-productive, and consequently irrational, to insist on the foundationalist belief that a methodology must ensure absolute truth before further steps can be taken. According to Nickles, the function of an adequate methodology is to generate relevant knowledge rather than the strangulation of that which falls short of certitude. 'It is a mistake', he argues, 'to say that the success or failure of a method is explainable only in terms of the truth of its substantive propositions. In fact, we often learn more rapidly by starting from contrary-to-fact assumptions about the world, rather than the most realistic assumptions. This just illustrates how a premature and priggish concern for the truth can block off the road to inquiry'.(ibid, p.124)

Because heuristic restrictors are not guarantors of truth they may, on occasion, eliminate paths that could lead to fruitful solutions. There is nothing new in this. Expert knowledge, even when linked to a truth-maximising methodology, is frequently cited as being responsible for putting a brake on the development of promising research. A chess heuristic may instantly remove from further consideration any move that left the queen under attack. This would be an excellent rule of thumb for a novice, but would occasionally lead the player to miss a rare opportunity for a winning queen sacrifice.

The account of discovery in terms of problem solving procedures aided by heuristic regulators can be misleading if it is assumed that the relationship between problem and solution is static. Whilst an understanding of the problem enhances solution-generation it is not uncommon for solutions to transform the problem. It is not unknown for solutions to await the appropriate problem. The drug 'Interferon' is such an example. In 1980 the microbiological firm, Biogen, announced that it had achieved the bacterial production of human interferon which, it was believed, would act as an antiviral agent and could be effective against cancer. There was an immediate flurry of research interest yet within six months it became apparent that Interferon was only marginally superior to existing therapy and even less effective against some cancers. In 1984 Interferon was described by Hillel Panich as a 'miracle cure in search of a disease' (cited by Longino, 1989, p.87). Strictly speaking, however, solutions do not emerge ahead of problems. Interferon was an inadequate solution to the original problem of combatting cancer which awaits application to a relevant disease.

Very frequently a problem will require modification before an acceptable solution can be applied. Problem transformation is equally as important as solution generation. The role of heuristics in problem transformation has not been fully appreciated. During periods involving conceptual shifts and reassessment of data, heuristic constraint may focus attention more sharply on certain details which were previously ignored. It is often the case, during an epistemological re-evaluation, that some key facts and theories are excluded by the new heuristic despite their obvious significance. One of the problems Aristotelian physics raised for Copernicanism was that according to the available data one could deduce that if the Earth actually rotated there should be an approximately 1,000 mile an hour counter wind. No such wind was detected. But in the early stages of the Copernican revolution this problem was ignored. Only later was it shown that it was Aristotelian physics, rather than Copernicanism, which lacked appropriate explanatory power. In the initial stages the new heuristic simply blocked off incompatible facts and theories. This might be productive, but the price is usually a loss of the explanatory power given by the earlier conceptual framework. Richard M. Burian (1987, p.12) poses this problem squarely:

> The fact must be faced that, at least in the short term, scientific progress is very often purchased at the price of a loss of explanatory breadth and power. That is, scientific 'progress' is often achieved by ignoring, or dismissing as irrelevant to the evaluation of current theories, facts which ought to be accounted for according to previously prevalent standards not specifically shown wrong.

Whilst seeking solutions to problems, the information required to select the most promising paths and eliminate others may only become available as the search progresses. One might not have a fully worked out set of heuristics at the outset. Solutions to problems may not appear ready at the outset of the inquiry and the problem itself may be transformed either in the early stages of its articulation or later during investigation. Problems are not static entities but are themselves transformed in the process of the search. Medical researchers might see the need for a cheaper and easier form of cardiac therapy as a problem which, in the course of researching it, may be transformed into a series of problems concerning diet and exercise.

A thorough examination of a problem may produce clues of the 'warm-cool' variety which will themselves guide the further conduct of the search. The game 'Twenty Questions', which was popular among listeners to post-war BBC radio, provides a good example of directed search and problem transformation. Peirce summarised the essential features of the game over half a century before its popularity through radio.

The game of twenty questions is instructive. In this game, one party thinks of some individual object, real or fictitious, which is well known to all educated people. The other party is entitled to answers to any twenty interrogatories they pronounce which can be answered by Yes or No, and are then to guess what was thought of, if they can. If the questioning is skilful, the object will invariably be guessed; but if the questioners allow themselves to be led astray by the will-o-the-wisp of any prepossession, they will almost as infallibly come to grief. The uniform success of good questioners is based upon the circumstance that the entire collection of individual objects well known to all the world does not amount to a million. If, therefore, each question could bisect the possibilities, so that yes and no were equally provable, the right object would be identified among a collection numbering 2^{20}. Now the logarithm of 2 being 0.30103, that of which its twentieth power is 6.30103, which is a logarithm of about 1,000,000 $(1 + .02 \times 2.3)$ $(1 + .0006 \times 2.3)$ or over one million and forty seven thousand, or more than the entire number of objects from which the selection has been made. Thus, twenty skilful hypotheses will ascertain what two hundred stupid ones might fail to do. The secret of the business lies in the caution which breaks a hypothesis up into its smallest logical components, and only risks one of them at a time. What a world of futile controversy and of confused experimentation might have been saved if this principle had guided investigations. (Peirce, 1931-1958, 7, p.220)

The essential feature of the game of 'Twenty Questions' was that each question limited the range of further questions. For example, in the search for the identity of the mystery object the first questioner might ask whether it was animal, vegetable or mineral. If the answer was 'animal', then further speculations about machines, rivers, and various artifacts, would be instantly blocked off. As more clues are analysed the scope of possibilities narrow down. In a significant sense, scientific innovators play the Twenty Questions game. Newton once said that the reason he could see further than others was because he 'stood on the shoulders of giants'. Among the giants who had asked some of the crucial regulative questions were Kepler, Galileo, Descartes and Hooke. Without Kepler's discovery that the planes of all possible orbits pass through the centre of the Sun, and Hooke's suggestions regarding the analysis of curved motion, Newton would have had less direction for the theory of universal gravity. Fortunately Newton did not have to watch fifty billion apples falling from trees before he arrived at a plausible hypothesis.

Heuristics and Problem-Solving

Examples of sophisticated problem solving systems are the DENDRAL and Meta-DENDRAL programs at Stanford University which use heuristic searches for hypothesis formation in organic chemistry. (Buchanan, 1969, 1985) These programs attempt to obtain a chemical structure formula from the experimental data from mass spectrograms of chemical compounds. Whilst the chemical formula is supposed to be known, the actual structure remains to be determined. But even for very simple organic compounds the valence-theoretically possible structures may involve many thousands of structural formulae. Each of these thousands is a 'hypothesis' and the desired result is the most plausible in the light of evidential data. The program is designed, as best as possible, to imitate the work of a human chemist. Its operation involves an attempt to reduce the number of acceptable hypotheses on the basis of the spectral data. For example, some structures assume the existence of certain sub-groups of atoms that precludes certain spectral lines. If the precluded spectral peaks do exist, the assumed structure is infirmed and the hypothesis is refuted. On the other hand, the existence of certain spectral peaks may be consistent with certain types of substructure, which offers a degree of confirmation. But the program also excludes structures which are unstable. This knowledge about stability and instability is part of the background knowledge and experience in chemistry, which is distinct from the 'evidence', which is the spectrum of the substance here. The program proceeds by means of a rejection of a large number of hypotheses so that in the final stage only a few will have survived the scrutiny.

In order to function on similar lines to a human chemist the program contains a considerable amount of extra-evidential considerations. Commenting on DENDRAL and meta-DENDRAL, B.G. Buchanan (1985) points out that they are based on a heuristic search method whose fundamental assumption is that discovery is a process involving the systematic exclusion of all implausible hypotheses. But this is only possible within a given framework, or paradigm, containing background scientific knowledge (and uncertain knowledge) of a given domain, which will help to define criteria for plausibility.

The role of heuristics in problem solving processes is best seen in activities or games involving complex choices. In chess, as we have seen, there are so many possible moves that even the best players can only contemplate a fraction of the possibilities. Before making a move a player might construct an imaginative picture of how the board will look after the move is made. This picture will provide a guide as to which moves are favourable or unfavourable, and what further moves are likely to be made by the opponent. Now the difference between the good player and the novice is not that the former has her head full of millions of possible moves more than the novice. The difference lies in the possession of a superior heuristic with which the good player eliminates useless moves. Given that even the best players can only handle a few possible continuities the skill lies in the ability to eliminate alternative moves without missing important possibilities. A chess master's heuristic eliminates as obviously useless certain moves which a novice might consider worthy of pursuit. Armed with a superior heuristic clues that the untrained cannot detect are obvious to the expert. For the experienced safe-cracker the 'clicks' he notices, although inaudible to the novice, are 'loud and obvious to him'. (Newell et al, 1967, p.82)

But how is a superior heuristic attained? There are no absolute guidelines. A minimum requirement would be a deep understanding of the problem, a knowledge of previous failures and fruitful clues, and considerable experience in the subject. An experienced farmer might know 'at a glance' which crop is most suitable for this soil - although he may not be able to articulate why, as he may not be consciously aware of his heuristics. A novice farmer may waste many seasons eliminating useless alternatives.

If scientific discovery is primarily a process of acquiring and applying heuristics to problem solving then what Koestler and others depict as the 'Aha reaction' is not so much an insight into any mysterious and irrational power, but simply the awareness of, or 'the acquisition of an additional piece of heuristic'.(Newell et al, 1967, p.96) Among the heuristics examined by Newell et al, are processes for working backwards from the solution; selection heuristics; functional means-end analysis, and planning. These, it is maintained, can all be simulated by computer programs. But as we shall later argue, analogies, metaphors, and models, whether amenable to computer simulation or not, provide important regulative heuristics in scientific research. Creativity, on these terms, is facilitated by techniques of solution restraint. The ultimate success of a problem solver rests primarily on an ability to make a correct selection from a very small part of the total problem solving maze for exploration. This approach conflicts sharply with conventional wisdom which emphasises a need to expand consciousness and multiply hypotheses. The latter, we have argued, collapses into an irrational brute force search. The point can be illustrated with reference to that supreme problem solver and master of heuristics, Sherlock Holmes.

Arthur Conan Doyle's A Study in Scarlet throws light on what we shall refer to as 'Holmes' heuristic'; that is, the sleuth's method of structuring information and reducing the search space. Watson, who has just made his first acquaintance with Holmes, is amazed at the latter's ignorance of Copernican theory. But Holmes justifies his ignorance as follows.

> 'You see', he explained, 'I consider that a man's brain originally is like a little empty attic, and you have to stock it with such furniture as you choose. A fool takes in lumber of every sort that he comes across, so that the knowledge which might be useful to him gets crowded out, or at best jumbled up with a lot of other things, so that he has difficulty in laying his hands upon it. Now the skilful workman is very careful indeed as to what he takes into his brain-attic. He will have nothing but the tools which help him in doing his work, but of these he has a very large assortment, and all in the most perfect order. It is a mistake to think that that little room has elastic walls and can distend to any extent. Depend upon it there comes a time when for every addition of knowledge you forget something that you knew before. It is of the highest importance, therefore, not to have useless facts elbowing out the useful ones'. (Conan Doyle, 1981, p.21)

Any reader of Conan Doyle will be aware that Holmes was not making out a case for ignorance and his remarks on the inelasticity of the brain should only be taken metaphorically: it is not the limitation of the data that produces the results but the criteria employed for its restriction.

One of the most exciting tasks for philosophers of science is the assessement of the influence and scope of heuristic principles in the regulation of scientific thinking, and the classification of them into distinct types for evaluation of their respective merits and weaknesses. (Nickles, 1989) Among the more obvious heuristic principles are the following:

1.   Universal assumptions regarding nature in general, such as principles of causality.

2.   Adopted scientific theories with greater explanatory power over their rivals, such as Newton's, Darwin's, and Einstein's respective theories.

110

3. Metaphysical frameworks, such as mechanism or vitalism.

4. Scientific values, such as those which stress avoidance of contact with pseudo-scientific theories, which instantly block off paranormal and telepathic explanations.

5. Ethical restraints, which prohibit use of data derived from immoral and inhumane experiments.

6. Economic restraints, awareness of prohibitive costs and of programs which may be financially supported.

One of the key features of heuristic directed search is the background knowledge which determines what is plausible and what is not. Like Holmes the detective, Linus Pauling the scientist, suggests that the key to successful problem solving is the elimination of useless facts, although, it would seem, he prefers a wider search space than the former.

> So what I'm saying is, its important to have a big background of knowledge. Also to do a lot of thinking. Probably part of the secret of being successful in a field involving discovery is the sort of judgement that keeps you from working in the wrong direction. A student once asked me, 'Dr Pauling, how do you go about having new ideas?' and I answered, 'You have to have a lot of ideas, and you throw away the bad ones. (Pauling, 1977)

Like Holmes, Pauling was speaking of a heuristic directed search. But as Buchanan pointed out in a discussion on the DENDRAL program, the criterion for selectivity depends on the level of background knowledge in any given domain. For Buchanan (1985, p.110) heuristics are only as reliable as conventional knowledge, and he concedes that 'putting confidence in the heuristics requires an act of faith'. On these terms this still leaves open the question of finding the best hypothesis restrictors. According to Buchanan, heuristic restraint only works within a background of Kuhnian 'normal science'. Revolutionary discoveries, involving superior heuristics, it would seem, remain as difficult to explain as they do for Popper and Reichenbach, and other exponents of the two-context theory. For Buchanan (ibid, p.111) a new and superior heuristic cannot be subjected to rational assessment.

In the most creative heights of science, hypothesis formation, is farthest from the 'search of method', as Whewell says. But within the comfort of an established theory, paradigm, or conceptual scheme, hypothesis formation usually does not involve the introduction of new concepts.

In this respect Buchanan moves closer to Kuhn, for whom revolutionary discoveries involve a different language which determines the evidential content of the paradigm. Thus to speak of light as travelling determines the kind of questions we can ask about light and the kind of answers we can expect, and the kind of hypotheses relating to it that can be ruled out as implausible. But in moments involving paradigm shifts there would be no rational means of moving from one paradigm to another.

It is this alleged confinement of heuristic search to a given theoretical context that is seen by critics as a limitation to computer based discovery programs. Carl Hempel (1985, p.118) sees the limits to computer based programs (and hence a logic of discovery) as follows: first, the limitation of all discoverable hypotheses to sentences expressible with the logical means of a given computer language; second, limitations on the available vocabulary to one that is antecedently given and fixed; third, limitations on the available principles of manifestation (more generally: limitations on the given empirical background). Hempel's point is that computer programs are severely limited in their power to generate novel hypothetical structures by the language in which the generator is written. A computer program might be able to envisage all possibilities in terms of permutations, but cannot postulate new terms or advance explanations beyond the existing framework of rules. Hempel (ibid, p.120) points out that a computer could not have generated new concepts by means of which oxygen theory replaced phlogiston theory.

The new concepts introduced by a theory of this kind cannot, as a rule be defined by those previously available; they are characterised by means of a set of theoretical principles linking the new concepts to each other and to previously available concepts that serve to describe the phenomena to be explained. Thus the discovery of an explanatory theory for a given class of occurrences requires the introduction both of new theoretical terms and of new theoretical principles. It does not seem clear at all how a computer might be programmed to discover such powerful theories.

Hempel raised these objections in the context of a discussion on the role of diagnostic computer programs, of which more will be said in Chapter V. His point is that none of the present diagnostic programs, such as INTERNIST-I and its successors, CADUCEUS and MYCIN, can diagnose novel diseases. If, for example, a patient had the signs and symptoms of Legionnaire's disease prior to the inclusion of data on the disease, then the program could not diagnose it. For no program, as yet, can generate the concept of a new disease.

In this respect Hempel's account of the limitations of computer discovery programs can be expressed in a Kuhnian distinction between discoveries in normal science and revolutionary discoveries. On this view computer discoveries are confined to modes of normal science and computer programs cannot generate those kinds of discoveries which transcend the limitations of the paradigm. Says Hempel (1985, pp.121-122):

> Indeed, in discovering hypotheses that are expressible in a language with fixed logical structure and fixed vocabulary, computers with an ingenious heuristic program, a large memory, high speed, and great reliability of performance will be able to out perform a scientist, and in some cases, no doubt, have already done so.

But when the search is aimed at comprehensive theories which require the introduction of a new vocabulary and the formation of theoretical principles in terms of it, then it is not clear how a suitable computer program might be designed.

It might be noted that the same criticism that Hempel makes about computer programs applies equally to scientists working within a Kuhnian paradigm. They too, allegedly work in a research space where the parameters are closely circumscribed and there is no scope for the generation of a new vocabulary. This view, however, rests on a rather narrow interpretation of Kuhn's account of scientific development and misses the fact that the language of any current paradigm is capable of transcending itself and reconstituting the entire problem domain. Nevertheless, it is difficult to construct in advance, either a new scientific paradigm or a computer program capable of so doing.

Despite Hempel's misgivings there are computer programs which could meet several of his objections concerning their ability to generate novel solutions. The revised discovery program, BACON-4, 'employs a small set of data driven heuristics to detect regularities in numeric and nominal data. These heuristics, by noting constances and trends, cause

BACON-4 to formulate hypotheses, define theoretical terms, postulate intrinsic properties, and postulate integral relations (common divisors) among qualities'. (Simon et al, 1981, p.12) According to Schaffner (1985, p.6) BACON-4 could generate novel discoveries, and meet Hempel's objection that new theoretical properties cannot be generated by computer-based discovery programs, as the program had one of its heuristics applied to data of the type that may have been available to Kepler and has actually generated Kepler's Third Law by compiling the data of the distance of the planets from the Sun and on the periods of their orbits.

So far neither BACON nor any other program has discovered anything new to it or to the world. However, there is no sharp dividing line between discovering things that are known by others and discovering things that are new to the world.

Notwithstanding its impressive abilities there is a sense in which it can be said that BACON only captures part of the problem solving activity crucial to many forms of scientific discovery, including some of Kepler's discoveries. Arthur I. Miller (1986, p.273) points out how the BACON program omits certain features of Kepler's research, such as his 'preoccupation with number mysticism and neo-Platonism, not to mention his idiosyncratic personality'. These aspects may or may not be important to computer simulation of problem solving but they can be responsible for the generation of various images, metaphors, analogies and metaphysical beliefs, which often structure a scientist's perception of a problem, and very often a solution will be generated by means of a conceptual transformation in this area. For example, Kepler would not have discovered his three laws without 'severe dramatic reconceptualisations of the problem domain'. (Holland et al, 1986, p.324) Much of his research was guided by metaphysical principles that would not be included in the BACON program. He held a geometric model of the planets as perfect solids with spherical orbits. Only with the adoption of a more physical model, which assumed that the Sun was - in some way - responsible for the motions of the planets, was progress made. Once freed from the geometric model Kepler was able to generate what he later called his First Law: that the motions of the planets are elliptical, with the Sun at the centre, rather than circular. In this respect Kepler developed his laws by a series of transformations of the mental models which, according to Holland et al, (ibid, pp.323-325) reveal the limitations of the BACON program as a representative of scientific discovery. Unlike BACON, Kepler was guided by mental models which assisted the transformation of his perception of the problem. Thus: 'Without his reconceptualisation of the motions of the planets into physical rather than geometrical terms, and his substitution of the notion of an ellipse for that of a circle, Kepler's achievements would have been impossible'. (ibid, p.325)

Any search for a solution will benefit from a heuristic which reduces the size of the problem space, but if Holland et al are correct, then search restriction is not enough; the direction provided by the mental model of the problem domain is equally necessary.

Other critics of computer simulation of creative problem solving have made similar points. Miller (1986, p.240) dismisses Simon's logic of discovery as 'a computerisation of Norwood R. Hanson's (1958) scenario of scientific discovery, which is closely connected to theories of perception'. Miller's objections are to Simon's 'pattern discovery' approach to the simulation of the discovery process. For, according to Miller, computers cannot reproduce aesthetic sensibility which is an important dimension of creative thinking. In contrast, Simon's account of computer simulation of the discovery process, on which the BACON program is modelled, is restricted to the detection of pattern regularities. As Simon (1977, p.33) reveals: 'Law detection means only finding patterns in the data that have been observed; whether the pattern will continue to hold for the new data that are observed subsequently will be decided in the course of testing the new law, not discovering it'.

Simon's account, argues Miller, fails to indicate how certain thinkers, such as Poincare, could see which mathematical facts were relevant or re-occurring. For in the case of Poincare's discovery of the Fuchsian functions it is unclear what the mathematical 'facts' that Poincare and his rival, Felix Klein, both 'saw' in 1881, but in which only Poincare could see the pattern statement that made the facts intelligible. Indeed, Poincare could not articulate a method for identifying useful facts beyond observing that they are 'simple', 'oft-recurring', and that it is 'the quest for this special beauty, the sense of harmony with the cosmos, which makes us choose the facts most fitting to contribute to this harmony'.(Miller, ibid, p.240)

The foregoing objections to the computer simulation of scientific discovery reveal, perhaps, some of the inadequacies in the exaggerated claims made by and on behalf of the Artificial Intelligentsia, but they are not in themselves damaging to the search for a logic of discovery. Models, metaphors, images and metaphysical beliefs, are clearly part of the apparatus of problem solving and may present problems for the computer simulation of discovery, but they are not insurmountable problems and do not provide support for the belief that discovery is resistant to rational assessment. Metaphysical beliefs may very well regulate scientific discovery but metaphysics can be taught, examined, and improved upon like any other heuristic. In any case discovery programs, such as DENDRAL and BACON, are not designed to actually reproduce the thought processes of particular scientists, but rather function in a limited sense as rational models of how discoveries might be made.

Routine and Revolutionary Problem Solving Processes

If we return to the question raised in the beginning of this chapter, of whether a different account of problem solving is required for periods of 'revolutionary science', we find that Kuhn speaks in this context of incommensurable paradigms and talking at cross-purposes. But even on his terms a different account of problem solving would not be required, because the problems of revolutionary science are also posed by normal science. They are the anomalous residual questions, which are left unanswered within the old paradigm, or impossible to reconcile with it. As such, new paradigms emerge from the gradual stream of scientific development - as Kuhn the historian portrays so excellently in his (1957) account of the Copernican Revolution. Just as a familiarity with the background knowledge of a paradigm is a necessary prerequisite for recognising and solving problems in normal science, so a familiarity with that which is deemed irreconcilable with the paradigm is a prerequisite for recognising and solving problems with novel or even revolutionary solutions.

There is, however, a sense in which serendipitous discoveries contribute to paradigm change, which raises the question whether the role of chance in scientific research can be cited in support of a distinction between routine and revolutionary discoveries. In a survey of serendipitous discoveries, which also outlines a version of evolutionary epistemology, Aharon Kantorovich and Yuval Ne'eman (1989) argue that whilst normal science resists analogies drawn with blind mutation in evolutionary theory, revolutionary discoveries necessarily involve blind variation. In normal science, they argue (ibid, p.507), problem solving is guided by a 'relatively stable world picture and conceptual system' and 'the prevailing tradition or heuristic partially guides scientists in the choice or in the construction of a hypotheses'. However, 'radical' or 'revolutionary' changes in science involve a very special class of 'blind variation'. This claim need not be invoked in support of romantic irrationalism as it simply recognises that serendipity (looking for one thing and finding something else) is part of the development of science in that an 'activity intended to solve a given problem leads to unintended results'. (ibid, p.512) In this respect a serendipitous discovery within the framework of normal science can 'destroy the prevailing order, and open up new vistas for science', by dragging the research programme in a new direction. (ibid, p.512)

116

The recognition of serendipity does not destroy the rationality of discovery, nor does it sustain the belief that a different mode of explanation is required for revolutionary discoveries. Scientists are not simple mechanisms tuned only to the recognition of one solution to one problem at a time. Seeking one thing (a sock) and finding another thing (a shirt) is a familiar event in all walks of life, and it should not be surprising to discover that science, too, develops in this manner. Attention to one problem will rarely block off solutions to other problems. Taking advantage of lucky finds is perfectly compatible with rational methods of hypothesis generation, even with regard to revolutionary hypotheses. The new is created by paying close attention to the old, taking advantage of serendipitous results derived from, and structured by, problems in normal science. Columbus, who was one of the most serendipitous discoverers of all time, did not conjecture without regulative heuristics.

The question whether or not discoveries made within periods of revolutionary science require a different explanation to those made in the context of normal science is clearly bound up with the distinction between revolutionary and normal science. On close examination it is a very hard distinction to maintain. The borderline is blurred by the fact that it is usually historians and philosophers, rather than practising scientists, who determine what a revolution is actually supposed to be. Moreover, changing fashions, reconstitutions, renaissances, the plundering of earlier work, and institutional requirements for emphasis on either continuity or rupture with the past, all blur the edges of the distinction. There are so many variables in the normal- revolutionary science distinction which make it difficult to square with reality. It is a logician's distinction and although it is useful for classifying and demarcating different groups of theories and related observations it cannot be cited in support of the thesis that revolution-making discoveries require a different explanatory framework to discoveries made in normal science.

The notion of logically distinct paradigms is certainly relevant to any assessment of the relationship between theory and data in different problem fields. But it does not warrant the postulation of historically water-tight boundaries which demarcate between different standpoints in a scientific revolution. William R. Shea (1987) offers a more interactionist model of paradigm replacement with reference to competing seventeenth-century theories of motion; the Cartesian Vortex theory and the Newtonian theory of universal gravity. According to Shea (1987, p.172): 'when different and rival explanations of the same phenomena are held, the defeated hypothesis is not always suppressed in a theoretical paradigm shift. It is often penetrated, infiltrated and transformed until it gradually passes into its technically superior rival ... an earlier theory can contain the seeds of a later one'. As Shea notes, the Vortex theory embodied two mechanical principles that Newton was to use, at least in the initial stages in the development of his own theory of motion; namely the principle of inertia and the concept of centrifugal force. The conceptual leaps postulated by a superficial interpretation of the Kuhnian theory of paradigm shifts are not instantaneous - despite Kuhn's flirtation with Gestalt-switch models and Kierkegaardian theories of religious conversion - in neither science nor politics. The tendency to percieve them as moments of radical discontinuity is more representative of a philosophical concern with dichotomous categories and neat logical divisions, rather than the historical development of ideas, reconstitutions and conceptual transformations.

It is rarely recognised that Popper, and others who argue against the possibility of a logic of discovery, does not draw a distinction between the respective contexts of discovery in normal science and revolutionary science. The opposition to a logic of discovery is designed to forestall *any* rational account of the context of discovery. But as Simon (1977, p.327) points out: 'If there is no such thing as a logical method of having new ideas, then there is no such thing as a logical method of having small new ideas'. Conversely, if there can be a logical method of having new small ideas then a logic of new ideas cannot be ruled out. If an account of a logical process for having new ideas, however small, can be given, then sufficient inroads into the two-context theory will have been made - unless its exponents provide a distinction between processes for generating routine and revolutionary new ideas. If, as it is argued here, there is no significant distinction between normal and revolutionary science, then arguments in favour of a logic of discovery are applicable to both.

This, of course, is not to deny that some discoveries are more important than others, with more impact on the scientific community, greater explanatory power, and so on. It is simply a rejection of the belief that revolution-making discoveries require some kind of special mode of understanding. According to the arguments advanced here the essential feature of creative and successful problem solving is the possession of a superior heuristic. This, however, invites the question, 'from where comes the superior heuristic?' There is a risk of circularity in the answer. It might be said that the superior heuristic is derived from the superior discoveries, but then the superior heuristic is responsible for the great discoveries and so, it would seem, there is no way out of the circle. This objection is not as damaging as it might first appear. The answer lies in the history of science. Most of the major discoveries have relied upon 'superior techniques of observation'. (Simon, 1977, p.291) In this respect Galileo's telescope, Leewenhoek's microscope, and Lawrences's cyclotron, are all examples of superior techniques of observation. But how did these 'superior' scientists come to possess superior techniques of observation? The answer is, by a combination of luck, persistence, and superior heuristics. This is not really as circular as it sounds. It is quite legitimate, argues Simon (ibid, p.291), when dealing with dynamic systems, to explain chickens by the hatching of eggs and eggs by the laying processes of hens. Popper could find little objection to this line of reasoning. As he observes when dealing with the question of which comes first, the hypothesis or the observation:

> The problem 'Which comes first, the hypothesis (H) or the observation (O)?' is soluble; as is the problem, 'Which comes first, the hen (H) or the egg (O)?' The reply to the latter is, 'An earlier kind of egg'; to the former, 'An earlier kind of hypothesis'. (Popper, 1963, p.47)

A case can be made for saying that the digital computer is associated with a superior technique in the sense that it can be applied to selective trial and error searches with considerable efficiency. Of primary importance is the background knowledge built into the software, awareness of blind alleys, previous failures and untried methods. Scientists are not like the monkeys in the British Museum; they have a background of beliefs, knowledge, and shared meanings. With equal background knowledge, when operating with a method of selective trial and error, all researchers are equal. For the greater part, scientific development is as equally dependent upon problem recognition - which includes the mental apparatus brought to the problem - as it is on the techniques for generating solutions.

It is often observed in computer studies that shortcomings in the solution are ultimately due to an inadequate characterisation of the problem. Elting E. Morison (1966, p.91) illustrates this with reference to one of Shakespeare's most infamous problem solvers.

> Hamlet had a problem which he defined for himself as follows: What happened to the late King of Denmark, and what should he, Hamlet, do about it? Framing the question accurately - a good program - he took it to a ghost, the most sophisticated mechanism in the late sixteenth-century for giving answers to hard questions. From the ghost he got back a very detailed reply which included a recommendation for a specific course of action. Responding to these advices, Hamlet created a political,

social, moral, and administrative mess that was simply hair raising.

The analogy with putting questions to computers is obvious, says Morison, ask a foolish question and the computer goes on answering the fool according to his folly. And in Hamlet's case: 'the trouble was that he had got the right answer, the answer to a question that was totally wrong. He had asked about his father when he should have asked, as any psychologist will tell you, about himself and his relations with his mother'. (ibid, p.91)

In the majority of cases involving creative problem solving it is simply a matter of asking the right questions. In periods described as normal science the right questions may be provided by the paradigm. A discovery that strains the very framework of the paradigm - a feature of scientific revolutions - does not come out of thin air; its genesis usually reveals a thorough familiarity with the paradigm to be transcended. The questions for revolutionary problem solvers, as are the questions for routine problem solvers, are provided by normal science which defines, for a time, what shall count as a legitimate area of research. The problems posed within normal science exhibit certain constraints which function as a kind of filtering mechanism for proposed solutions, even if the very problem itself is later transformed as new solutions generate a different problem field. These constraints are heuristic devices wherein problems virtually indicate their own solutions, thus indicating the narrowness of the margin between problem articulation and solution generation.

In recent years the pioneering work of Simon, Newell, and Langley, has been developed by philosophers who share the view that creative discovery is a rational procedure. In the following chapter the examination of a logic of discovery will be developed with reference to research work which brings together both solution generators and solution restricting processes as integral features of a logic of discovery.

V   Generation and evaluation

A Logic of Generation

Research in Artificial Intelligence on the simulation of human problem solving processes has focused on the interplay between solution generators and solution restrictors. The application of Artificial Intelligence research to computer diagnostic programs further demonstrates the possibility of a logic of discovery. Building on Simon and Newell's work in Artificial Intelligence, Kenneth Schaffner (1980, p.171) defined a logic of discovery as 'a set of well-characterised and applicable rules for *generating new knowledge*'. He defined a logic of justification as 'a set of rules for *assessing* or *evaluating* the merits of preferred claims about the world in the light of their purportedly supportive evidence'. In Schaffner's reformulation of the two-context theory, the traditional discovery-justification distinction was superseded by a distinction between 1) a logic of generation and 2) a logic of preliminary evaluation. Despite his support for Hanson's claims on behalf of a logic of discovery, Schaffner was ultimately critical of the former's failure to recognise these two essential aspects of the process of discovery. Said Schaffner (ibid, p.179):

> Hanson, in his far ranging writing on retroduction, never distinguished clearly between 1) a *logic of generation*, by which a new hypothesis is first articulated, and 2) a *logic of*

121

preliminary evaluation, in terms of which an argument is assessed for its plausibility.

Schaffner maintains that the fundamental weakness of Hanson's logic of discovery is its failure to earmark the logic of generation, the means of generating the hypothesis in the first place. Without a logic of generation 'the retroductive model of inference is little more than the H-D model itself'. (ibid, p.189) And without a rational account of hypothesis generation explanations of discovery collapse into the kind of account favoured by exponents of the two-context theory: irrational generation and deductive rejection.

An awareness of the respective functions of a logic of generation and a logic of preliminary evaluation, argues Schaffner, is also missing in Achinstein's and other accounts of retroductive logic. On Schaffner's terms the distinction between generation and preliminary evaluation is not equivalent to the inductive-deductive distinction. The task of a logic of generation, he says, 'is the production of new hypotheses'. Its function is to 'articulate heretofore unasserted conclusions'. (ibid, p.179) These may range from the strikingly original, through the moderately novel - as when standard ideas are put together in new ways in Koestler's bisociative context to solve a problem - to the trivial. Following Simon, Schaffner does not attribute any significance to a distinction between the routine and the more spectacular discoveries. A logic of generation need not be concerned with a qualitative assessment of new ideas or with any distinctions between the values placed upon their originality. There are, however, two senses in which a logic of generation can be depicted; the weak and the strong sense. The weak sense covers what is commonly seen as retroduction and also analogical reasoning. The strong sense would include traditional naive Baconian induction and ennumerative induction, and evocation in the logic of diagnosis. (ibid, p.180) A logic of evaluation involves an assessment of claims of support or entailment. It too has weak and strong claims. In the weak sense it would include retroduction, logic of comparative theory, Bayesian logic of non-statistical hypothesis testing, and proofs by approximation. In the strong sense it would include eliminative induction, statistical hypothesis testing, and certain inductive logics such as Carnap's. (ibid, p.180)

Schaffner sees both the generative and evaluative aspects of discovery as important components of the logic of discovery. Consequently, his account of generation and evaluation is intended to supersede the traditional discovery-justification distinction, insofar as both aspects are amenable to logical analysis. His motivation, then, is not to provide a demarcation line between the objects of philosophical and psychological inquiry, but to draw attention to two complimentary aspects of a logic of discovery. A fully developed logic of discovery, he argues (ibid, p.181), requires both a logic of generation and a logic of weak evaluation. Moreover, there are significant aspects of the discovery process which are constituted by the logic of preliminary or weak evaluation which need articulation. At present the logic of generation is restricted to non-novel solutions and is generally restricted to Artificial Intelligence studies and non-original hypotheses. But this should not be understated. When it involves cases where non-original hypotheses are taken in combination it can produce solutions which are difficult for experienced scientists to generate. In fact, this bringing together of non-original hypotheses is, in essence, Koestler's bisociative context stripped of its mystical trappings.

Triggering Conditions

Aspects of a logic of generation which need to be examined here are the triggering conditions which also act as rational constraints on hypothesis generation. In a multi-disciplinary study of processes of discovery John H. Holland, Keith J. Nisbet, Richard E. Thogard, and R. Paul (1986) cite two important kind of triggering conditions. The first is the failure of a prediction, and the second is the occurrence of some unusual event. In the case of a failed expectation the mechanism triggered will be 'specific to the difficulty, generating rules that are plausible repairs or additions to the active model'. (ibid, p.80) In the case of an unexpected event, a new heuristic 'may generate a limited range of new rules constituting hypotheses to accommodate the event'. (ibid, p.80)

Two familiar triggering mechanisms in these circumstances are abductive or retroductive reasoning and reasoning by analogy.

Abduction as a generator

Despite criticism of the logical status of abductive inference it is widespread in human thinking, in solving crimes, diagnosing diseases, and solving general problems. A doctor might reason abductively when she diagnoses a certain disease on the grounds that this disease provides the best explanation of the patient's symptoms. But abduction may also trigger off new generalisations. As Holland et al (1986, p.89) point out.

One important type of abduction involves the triggering of a new generalisation. Suppose an artist is late for a meeting. You may form the general rule that artists are usually late, because that rule plus the fact that the tardy acquaintance is a painter would provide an explanation of the lateness. The motive of the generalisation here is not just to summarise knowledge about a number of instances... but to produce an explanation. Abduction will often require search through the default hierarchy of relevant concepts to find the most appropriate explanatory hypothesis.

As the above example shows, abduction may generate various types of hypotheses, although many cases of abductive reasoning may vary in explanatory strength. In view of this Holland et al recommend that the best way to arrive at non-arbitrary hypotheses is by 'multiple abductions', so that explanations cover a variety of facts. (ibid, p.89) In this respect a partial reply to Achinstein's (1980) criticism of abduction can be proposed. For the wild hypothesis, considered by Achinstein, that the reason he was writing a book was that he had been promised a million dollars on completion, would not be considered in isolation. Other abductions would kill off the wilder and less plausible inferences.

Analogy as a generator

The role and status of analogical reasoning will be examined more closely in a later section. But it is appropriate to consider here the role of analogical inference as a solution generator. By use of analogies a model for a problem domain need not be built up from scratch, but can derive most of its structure from other successful models. Modern wave theories of light can be traced to the seventeenth century, when the analogy was drawn between sound and light. Sound travels at a finite velocity through a milieu, so does light. Thus in 1675 Roemer ascertained that light travels at a very fast, but finite, velocity. The milieu for light waves was initially conceieved of as the ether, which maintained the analogy with sound waves passing through the air, which in turn had been derived from analogies with water. These analogies provided instantly plausible models for further inferences. Their adoption placed a restriction on less plausible analogies: for example a 'ball theory of sound', whereby sound is conceived in terms of a series of minute moving balls, would be too awkward and unlikely to attract initial interest, and would meet difficulties in explaining how the 'bits' of sound could pass each other without interruption.

A problem may resist solution because it is ill-defined and requires a degree of transformation by means of an analogy. Holland et al (ibid, p.290) drew attention to what they describe as an analogical approach to the 'radiation problem', which consists in asking students the following question.

> Suppose you are a doctor faced with a patient with a malignant tumour in the stomach. An operation is impossible, but death will occur if the tumour is not destroyed. However, there is a ray that, at sufficient high intensity will destroy the tumour. But unfortunately at this rate of intensity the rays passing through other organs to the tumour will destroy healthy tissues. At lower intensities the tissues will not be harmed, but then the tumour will not be destroyed either. Problem: how can the rays be used to destroy the tumour without harming the healthy tissue?

As it stands the problem is ill-defined. For we do not have an adequate representation of the potential results of altered effects of the rays, nor any information regarding the means of decreasing the sensitivity of the healthy tissue or increasing the vulnerability of the tumour. The problem requires transformation, which can be done by means of analogy. The analogy introduced by Holland et al (ibid, p.291) is taken from an experiment by M.L. Gick and K.J. Holyoak (1980) who told students the following story in order to generate a solution to the radiation problem.

> A general wished to capture a fortress in the centre of a country. The roads radiating from the fortress were mined, such that small groups could pass over safely, any large group would detonate the mines. But to launch a successful attack the whole army had to get through to the fortress.

The problem now parallels that of the radiation problem, and probably poses it in a clearer setting. The following solutions were generated by means of this analogy.

1. The general discovers an unguarded route to the fortress and sends his entire army along it.

2. He divides his men into smaller groups sending them simultaneously down multiple routes to the fortress.

When we return these analogies to the radiation problem we find the following suggestions.

1. Send the rays down an 'open passage', such as the oesophagus, so as to reach the tumour without damaging nearby tissue. A more detailed suggestion involved the insertion of a 'ray proof' tube to avoid contact (since the oesophagus is not straight). This variant illustrates how analogies can be adapted once they are initially drawn.

2. Just as the general divides his forces, so a 'convergence solution' might involve the direction of multiple weak rays at the tumour from different directions.

Approximately 75% of the college students in the tests generated the convergence solution after hearing the military story. Only 10% did so without the assistance of a strong analogy.

The use of analogies as generators or triggering conditions, despite their obvious limitations, has proved successful in both science and the humanities, and a close examination of their function in creative work should demonstrate affinities between the two fields of inquiry. As Eugene Laschyk (1986, p.167) observes, one reason why science and the humanities have been perceived to be separable 'is that models, analogies, and metaphors have not received adequate attention in the past'.

Metaphors

The status of metaphor has fared badly in positivist philosophy of science. This is partly a legacy of the Enlightenment attempt to dispose of demons. As metaphor was part of the 'darkness of the mind' reason had to banish it. In the hands of the logical empiricists of the early twentieth century metaphor was relegated to poetry; it was merely emotive, devoid of scientific meaning. But metaphor need not be banished from scientific thought and can even be seen as an essential contribution to rational problem solving processes. Although a metaphorical account of a phenomenon may not guarantee conviction, a good metaphor may prove highly rewarding in the generation of ideas. Donald Schon's (1969) study of invention revealed how the possibility of generating new ideas out of earlier conceptual structures can be facilitated by close attention to the metaphors contained in earlier formulations. Schon (1969, p.95) suggested that 'it is worthwhile paying attention to the literal language in which theories are formulated', as it 'is often suggestive of metaphors underlying the theory and therefore worthy of further elaboration or examination of related metaphors yielding new hypotheses'.

Nevertheless, it is one thing to recognise the generative role of metaphors but admitting them as an integral feature of scientific research is viewed with suspicion. In general metaphors in scientific thought have not been seriously assessed by twentieth century philosophers of science, who frequently portray them as an external aspect of scientific research akin to poetic insight and, if valuable at all, reducible to propositions of factual discourse. One exception to this trend was the investigation of metaphors by the philosopher, Max Black (1962), who argued that metaphor is both an intrinsic and rational aspect of scientific research.

Black considered typical metaphorical statements such as 'Man is a wolf', and noted that the effect of describing man as a wolf was to evoke a network of features frequently attributed to wolves. Wolves are allegedly fierce and hungry; they are said to prey on other animals, they scavenge, and so on. The overall effect of this metaphor will be the construction of a system of new implications about men, depending on the aspects of wolf behaviour highlighted by the metaphor. According to Black (1962, p.41): 'any human traits that can without undue strain be talked about in "wolf-language" will be rendered prominent, and any that cannot will be pushed to the background. The wolf-metaphor suppresses some details, emphasises others - in short, organises our view of man'.

Thus conceived, metaphors involve bringing a system of classification to work in a new area. They enable us to draw from the knowledge held within the primary system of classification, which may be well established, and apply it to the secondary system in its generative phase. Thus by calling a man a wolf, lion, or reptile, we draw on a system of classification which has no literal role in the context of human classifications. Yet the metaphor may provide a new level of understanding about men. The use of metaphors facilitate the use of the power of the system from which they are borrowed. Metaphors are neither sloppy nor imprecise alternatives to rigorous argument. According to Black's interactionist account of metaphor a metaphorical statement has two distinct subjects; a principle subject and a subsidiary one. The metaphorical statement selects, emphasises, suppresses and organises features of the principle subject by implying statements about it which normally apply to the subsidiary subject. (Black, 1962, pp.44-5) In this way the metaphor facilitates the seeing of new connections. If, for example, a battle is described in metaphorical language derived from chess, the metaphor might suppress some features connected with the principle subject, such as the horror and carnage, and emphasise others, such as the tactics, planning and long term strategy. This could be changed by the use of metaphors referring to the battlefield as a 'butcher's block' or 'slaughter house', which would highlight other features of the principle subject. In choosing which aspects of the principle subject should be either emphasised or played down considerable precision may be required. This has been well-demonstrated in medical diagnosis where discourse concerning symptoms can prove fruitful if correct attention to metaphor is observed.

Metaphors function as bridges between disciplines, extending meanings from an established context to provide clarity in another. Although buildings do not blow saxaphones and beat drums they can be described as being 'jazzy', for the system of musical meanings can overlap with architecture. 'Loud' may be a literal description of a band, but it serves as an adequate metaphorical description of a neck-tie. It works as a metaphor because it brings the notion of excessiveness from one framework to another. (Goodman and Elgin, 1988) Metaphorical references to 'blowing off steam', 'getting wires crossed' and 'keeping the pressure up', all reveal the ease with which the human situation can be metaphorically depicted in a technical framework.

Science, no more than everyday experience, music or architecture, cannot avoid metaphors. In characterising the behaviour of sub-atomic particles one might describe how bosons are 'eaten' or 'absorbed' by other particles, how mesons 'knock' electrons off atoms. It is, of course, important to be aware of the limits of metaphors, just as it is important to be aware of the limits of any form of essential scientific equipment. This, however, does not mean that metaphors are sub-standard equipment, but rather that like computers, cyclotrons and slide rules, metaphors require expert handling.

The risk of misusing metaphors has led many philosophers of science into a conservative position from which they regard metaphorical discourse as having only a limited, even dispensible, role. Referring to the metaphors employed in sub-atomic physics Anthony O'Hear (1988, p.100) says:

> To speak, correctly, of such thinking as metaphorical is to assert that we know that gas molecules and atoms, bosons and mesons, are not *exactly* like that, and that we do not intend the comparisons to be taken literally...in science it becomes important to make precise the limits of the metaphor, to show just the respects in which an atom, say, is like and unlike a solar system. And once this is done, it is unclear how much of the metaphor actually remains, except as a device for introducing what are now precisely clarified ideas to a beginner.

While it is essential to limit the scope of metaphors, O'Hear's account implies that metaphors play only a pedagogical, and ultimately dispensible, role in scientific thinking. The view advanced here, in contrast, is that metaphors are essential regulatory aspects of solution generation, providing guidelines derived from established systems for venturing into new domains. Far from being dispensable pedagogic aids, they are part of the standard equipment of scientific research requiring professional skills for their selection, application and extension.

The view of metaphor as a working regulator finds expression in David Bohm and David Peat's (1988) reworking of Kuhn's portrayal of scientific revolutions. Creativity, they argue, is not confined to momentary revolutionary periods as Kuhn's (1970) model suggests, but is best understood in terms of the long-term 'unfolding of a metaphor'. According to Bohm and Peat metaphor is essential to creative discovery in that its unfolding can assist in bringing together theories hitherto regarded as incommensurable. It was, they argue, a metaphor which linked Newtonian theory to the seemingly incommensurable Hamilton-Jacobi wave theory, which was based on the idea of treating motion as waves rather than particles. The image of the movement of a stick carried by waves on a lake provided the metaphor of motion 'determined by waves a a whole, rather than by precise local actions of a force at each point in the trajectory of the particle'. (ibid, p.39) The calculations of wave theory generated the same mathematical results as particle theory, but scientists in the nineteenth century did not appreciate the full extent of this metaphor. Concentrating exclusively on the mathematical aspects of the new theory they regarded wave and particle theories as incommensurable alternatives. 'Had they grasped the full extent of the metaphor - a particle *is* a wave - they would have connected the two theories thus anticipating the modern quantum-mechanical notion of wave-particle duality'. (ibid, p.40) What are now required, say Bohm and Peat, are creative metaphors that will serve as bridges between quantum theory and relativity theory.

The claim that scientific language should contain metaphors, and that metaphor functions as an important regulative research instrument, may be an anathema to positivist philosophers of science who can only accept metaphor insofar as it is located outside rational discourse. But metaphors are not extraneous aspects of human discourse and scientific research actually requires them. Furthermore metaphors are rational insofar as they have a rationale, that is, when we can find reasons for using them, and when they can be tested and assessed (i.e. to see if they fit). The assessment of metaphors is an important role for philosophers of science and linguists who could trace out their implications, their negative and positive features, and consider the relevance of combining hitherto unrelated systems.

Analogies

Analogies are very powerful in scientific thought and probably generate and regulate more ideas than any other mode of thinking. Yet like metaphorical discourse appeals to analogy have a low status among contemporary philosophers of science. Even so, despite its weak status analogical reasoning is given a significant, although morally controversial, role in the sense that it provides scientific credibility for the results derived from animal experimentation and vivisection.

Francis Bacon insisted that one of the requisites of scientific ability was 'a mind nimble and versatile enough to catch the resemblance of things which is the chief point and yet at the same time steady enough to fix and distinguish their subtler differences'. (cited by W.H. Leatherdale, 1974, p.13) In a similar vein Sir Humphrey Davy argued that: 'a rapidity of combination, a power of perceiving analogies, and of comparing them by facts, is the creative source of discovery'. (cited by Leatherdale, 1974, p.13) The seventeenth-century mechanistic concept of the universe was based on an analogy with a clock. Robert Boyle went so far as to find evidence for God's existence in the analogy between clockwork regularity and cosmic uniformity when he described the universe as being 'like a rare clock...where all things are so skilfully contrived, that the engine being once set a-moving, all things proceed according to the artificer's first design'. (Boyle, 1772, v.163) Hume, however, disposed of the design argument which others derived from this analogy, but the force of the clockwork analogy as a model for the universe should not be underestimated in that it exerted sufficient power to replace previous animistic models of the universe with the mechanistic world view.

Nevertheless, like metaphors, analogies have to be treated with caution. Hume's devastating attack on the argument from design, in *The Dialogues Concerning Natural Religion*, warns of the dangers of analogical reasoning. His account is largely responsible for its relatively low status in the philosophy of science. Karl Marx, also, drew attention in *Capital* to the way analogies may inhibit technological progress. He referred to the way mechanical locomotion may well have been delayed through attempts to construct self propelling vehicles with feet instead of wheels, a piece of folly due to the strength of the analogy between machines and living organisms. Progress was made when the analogy was broken; in nature wheels have not evolved. Finally, is Peirce's (1957, p.134) warning that 'there is no greater nor more frequent mistake in practical logic than to suppose that things that resemble one another strongly in some respects are any more likely for that to be alike in others'.

Analogical reasoning has been an extremely fruitful source of hypothesis generation with built-in regulative heuristics. From evidence derived from telescopic observations which showed that the Sun, Venus, and Saturn move, Galileo argued that by analogy the Earth moves. Pushing the analogy further he argued that since Saturn moves and has a moon that moves around it, therefore the Earth which has a moon that moves around it, must also move. Today the force of such a weak analogy escapes the modern reader, but for seventeenth-century thinkers it was a plausible generator in a process of reasoning which led to the adoption of the heliocentric theory.

Notwithstanding Marx's reservations regarding the analogy between living organisms and machines, Harvey's successful attempt to understand the blood system was based on an analogy between a water pump and the heart. His concept of hydraulics had shared aspects with certain living organisms, such as the fact that the blood flows through tubes, will spurt out if the tubes are broken, and is pumped through tubes at considerable pressure. The analogy was further confirmed by observations at various stages: venous valves were observed which were only consistent with one-direction blood flow; and muscles of the heart were observed to be responsible for the motor pump action.

As a rule the force of successful analogies depends upon the perception of similarities between the structure of problems solved and problems yet unsolved. But sometimes analogies may have a broader and more metaphysical significance, as in the case of the holographic analogy formulated by Karl Pribram, David Bohm, and K. Wilber. (1982) According to the holographic analogy there are significant similarities between each individual and the whole universe, which is indicative of 'an intimate relationship between human intelligence and the intelligibility of the universe'.(Bohm and Peat, 1988, p.149) The expression 'holographic analogy' is bound up with the fact that a small part of a holographic photograph will nevertheless reproduce the complete image of the whole subject, rather than a fragment of it. The analogy has come to represent a unification of research in disciplines as remote from each other as physics and neurophysiology, with the regulative belief that 'looking inward' at the individual, is the same as 'looking outward' at the universe. Drawing out this analogy would (for some of its exponents) bring out similarities between Eastern metaphysics and Western physics.

Analogies function primarily in the field of invention. Close scrutiny of the structure and function of the wings of bats and birds have provided useful analogies for aircraft designers. But progress depends on limiting these analogies. No aeroplane wing could ever be an exact copy of a bat's wing. The extent and limitation of the analogy is either modified by the researcher's background knowledge of scientific laws and accumulated wisdom or is discovered later as the analogy is developed. As both generative and regulative devices analogies are essential pieces of scientific equipment which can be carefully scrutinised, and their limitations revealed. For example, one of the most breathtaking analogies in modern physics was Bohr's model of the atom. As Max Born observed:

> A remarkable and alluring result of Bohr's atomic theory is the demonstration that the atom is a small planetary system..., the thought that the laws of the microcosmos in the small field reflect the terrestrial world obviously exercises a great magic on mankind's mind; indeed its form is so rooted in the superstition (which is as old as the history of thought) that the destiny of men could be read from the stars. The astrological mysticism has disappeared from science, but what remains is the endeavour toward the knowledge of the unity of the laws of the world.(Born, cited by Arthur Miller, 1986, p.129)

He concluded that the analogy between the atom and a planetary system has limitations in that it only works strictly in the case of the hydrogen atom.

Following Mary Hesse (1970) analogies can be examined with reference to their negative and positive features. For example, Norman Robert Cambell's account of the dynamical properties of gases - the kinetic theory of gases - was based on an analogy between the random motion of a collection of billiard balls and the movement of a gas's molecules. The kinetic theory of gases gave fairly accurate predictions that gas laws would break down under high pressure, because the 'balls' would push up against each other such that they could not move as freely as they would in 'ideal gas' conditions. As Hesse (1970, p.8) points out, when drawing such an analogy one is not saying that the billiard balls function in every respect as models for the gas molecules. Some properties of the gas molecules are not found in billiard balls. Those properties which are not found in billiard balls constitute the *negative* analogy of the model, whereas motion and impact would be described as the *positive* analogy of the model.

When reasoning with analogies it is therefore essential to assess the respective balance between their negative and positive features. Consider the analogy between the Earth, the Moon, and Venus. In terms of their common physical features they are large, solid, opaque, spherical bodies receiving heat and light from the Sun, revolving on their axes, and gravitating towards other bodies. (Hesse, ibid, p.58) These properties constitute a positive analogy. But the Moon is smaller than the Earth, more volcanic, and has no water. In this respect there are negative aspects of the analogy between the Earth and the Moon, which are initially stronger than those between the Earth and Venus with regard to inquiries concerning the possibility of life-forms on either the Moon or Venus. In this example the negative aspects of the analogy functions as a solution restrictor.

The concept of the genetic code provides a good example of both the generative and heuristic power of analogy. Yet it also reveals the need for caution with regard to the negative and positive features of such reasoning. In his study of the role of rhetoric in science Alan G. Gross (1990, p.25) points out that 'just as a code conveys information from one human being to another, a genetic code transfers genetic information from the hereditary substance to the protein that forms living matter'. But as Gross insists this analogy was heuristic rather than probative for whilst it 'led Crick to the correct interpretation of the structure of DNA (it) also led him to the incorrect formulation of the way the genetic code was read'. (ibid., p.30) Crick's errors in reading the code were later outlined by Marshall W. Nirenberg and his colleague, J. Heinrich Matthaei, who, working with the same analogy - stressing its positive features - discovered the correct formulation (ibid.).

Reasoning by means of analogy may not be conclusive but it is clearly rational in the sense that good reasons may be given for using them. As generative and regulative devices they are an integral feature of scientific research. A central argument in Darwin's *Origin of the Species* is the analogy between artificial breeding and natural selection. But this analogy was more than a generative device, certainly more than a pedagogic aid: 'it was not abandoned as the theory matured; instead, it was the means by which the theory has been maintained and extended'. (Gross, 1990, p.18) Analogies are not inferior modes of reasoning; they are central to the very meaning of science. 'Laboratory experiments', says Gross (ibid, p.18) 'are scientifically credible only if there is a positive analogy between laboratory events and processes in nature'. Like other indispensible scientific instruments analogies perform best when applied by skilled minds aware of their limitations. Like laboratory instruments they can be examined, scrutinised, improved, or rejected with good reason.

Models

Numerous discoveries have been enhanced by successful models which have generated novel predictions such that when they are observed the theory gathers force. The discovery in 1919, that light is bent when it passes over large bodies was an outcome of a model developed out of Einstein's

General Theory of Relativity. Models help to highlight some aspects of reality whilst excluding others. Thus Marxism employs models which highlight the economic base as a determinant of a culture to the exclusion of other factors; Freudianism takes sexual urges to the exclusion of others, and Darwinism focuses on competition to the exclusion of other features of biological phenomena. The employment of models is clearly double-edged. Whilst it may be beneficial to exclude some aspects of reality for the purpose of investigation a too rigid exclusion may lead to impoverished results and exaggerated claims on behalf of the theory derived from them.

Models, like metaphors, have been either dismissed or portrayed as external features of scientific investigation. But as Black (1962, p.236) argues: 'models are sometime not epiphenomena of research, but play a distinctive and irreplaceable part in scientific investigation; models are not disreputable understudies for scientific formulas'. It will be argued here that models are generative and regulative features of scientific work. They are not meant to be faithful representations of reality: like metaphors they suppress some aspects and emphasise others. A scale model of a train offers only selected features of the original. In this respect it manifests both negative and positive features of the original. One important negative feature would be derived from a background knowledge about scaling, which would regulate predictions concerning the quantitative difference of damage occurring in collision or impact with scaled down models and actual trains. A train which plunges down a thirty foot embankment will suffer far greater damage than a scaled down model subjected to a similar impact.

As well as the rigour and precision which mathematics brings to scientific thinking, mathematics provides very powerful models. Its abstract nature adds an extra dimension to solution generation which often transcends empirical experience. Yet when a theory is represented mathematically, it still functions as a model of reality; it simply highlights aspects which might be obscured in a physical representation.

Models vary in kind and function, highlighting some aspects of a problem and excluding others. Apart from scale models and mathematical models there are various theoretical models of the 'as if' form (as if it were filled with a material medium) where ontological commitment is temporarily suspended. Other models might be construed as real representations, as were E. Rutherford's solar system and Bohr's model of the atom of which it has to be concluded that these were presented as descriptions of the atom as it really is. One of the precursors of the 'plate techtonics' revolution in the earth sciences, Alfred Wegener, was initially guided in his thinking on continental drift theory by observations of glaciers, ice-flows and icebergs, which 'provided him with valuable models, and a rich source of metaphors for large masses moving imperceptibly accross the surface of the earth'. (Giere, 1988, p.230) Critics of Wegener in the 1920's, however, rejected the model largely because of the absence of any plausible mechanism for continental drift.

In many cases models function as idealisations which limit attention to one area of solution space. For example, a traffic engineer studying the movement of a city's transport system might make a model wherein each vehicle is represented by a small rectangular block. The negative features of the analogy between the model and reality might be the design of each vehicle, its engine size and distribution of weight, which will have been excluded from the representation. For at issue here is only traffic flow and how congestion can be relieved. In such cases the omission of certain facts may not invalidate the results of the study; the model simply directs attention away from irrelevant details. What are ignored here are levels of reality which are deemed to be irrelevant to the kind of solution that is desired, although it may well be the case that another inquiry will see them in a more positive light.

The use of models as solution generators and regulators is a recognition that there can be no such thing as a perfect comprehensive representation of reality. Unnecessary details just have to be omitted. The Earth is more or less spherical, but plans for the building of a house do not have to record this fact. Models, like plans, offer satisficing rewards; they are 'good enough' for the task in hand if their limitations are clearly set out.

Diagnosis and Discovery

One of the most promising research sites for investigation into the logic of generation and evaluation is current work on computer diagnostic programs. Some of the more interesting work in this area is based on attempts to simulate the thought processes of experienced clinicians rather than the mere use of computers for brute force search methods. (Schaffner, 1985) The process of medical diagnosis is sufficiently rich and complex to serve as a model for creative discovery. Both discovery and diagnosis have been wrongly characterised as irrational, instinctive processes, closer to wizardry than to rational investigation. Like many scientists who subscribe to the two-context theory, there are physicians who depict diagnosis as an art, or as something requiring little more than 'good sense', and believe that if there were a logic of diagnosis it would have to consist of foolproof rules for the guarantee of correct diagnoses on every occasion. Since the latter does not exist, it is widely held that diagnosis is ultimately beyond the scope of rational assessment. In reply it should be stressed that absolute certainty is never achieved in either science or medicine, although in the latter case some degree of certainty can be obtained by an autopsy when the pathologist may confirm what the disease actually was. For the most part, discovery and diagnosis deal with the next best thing to certainty; good reasons for proposing and adopting a hypothesis.

Like the processes involved in scientific discovery, diagnostic processes have solution generators and solution restrictors. In diagnosing diseases the notion of a 'prior probability' can function as a search restrictor. For example, if an influenza bug is rampant in the neighbourhood and a patient complains of fever and chills, the prior probability is that the patient has influenza. This probability would be high, even if it turned out that the patient had either tuberculosis or malaria. To ignore prior probability would be to resort to a mindless brute force search where *every* disease is regarded with equal probability. This might improve chances of detecting the occasional rare disease but would seriously inhibit the diagnosis and treatment of more common diseases, as a brute force search, from the start, would be necessary in every case.

There may be another set of prior probabilities concerning those situations where the same symptoms could refer to another disease. These naturally reduce the former set of prior probabilities. These two sets of prior probabilities will then figure largely in the physician's mind during the initial stages of the diagnosis. Further data gleaned from the patient and the physician's mental library will help both generate and eliminate other hypotheses. This is not blind art or intuition, but (admittedly) a grossly simplified version of a rational process of selection which can be assisted by means of Bayesian theory.

Research in the logic of diagnosis has received considerable impetus from work on computer diagnostic programs. (Schaffner, 1980, 1985) Many of these programs simply follow the canons of a strict Popperian methodology: generate hypotheses and falsify them deductively. But such schemes are idealisations, because there is no error free rule (according to the Popperian standpoint) for the elimination of hypotheses. The further question is (and this is where we part company with Popper) which is the most plausible (i.e. rational) way of generating and restricting hypotheses?

At the University of Pittsburgh in 1974 Jack Myers (an internist) and Harry Pople (a computer scientist) first succesfully demonstrated INTERNIST-I, a diagnostic program in internal medicine, which utilised the techniques of Artificial Intelligence. Since then it has been used in the analysis of hundreds of clinical problems, and improvements to the program continue. Current research has led to many refinements to the program, and to its successor, CADUCEUS. INTERNIST-I has an extensive knowledge base of about five hundred diseases and over three thousand disease manifestations known to internal medicine, which are arranged in a hierarchy from the general to the specific. Each disease is characterised by a disease profile, which is a list of manifestations, (i.e., signs and symptoms) history, and laboratory data associated with the disease. In addition to the disease file are a number of 'links' between certain diseases which are meant to capture the degree to which one disease may relate to another, such as the derivibility of one disease from another. (Pople, 1985)

One of the early problems with INTERNIST-I was bound up with the need to discern multiple diseases in an individual patient. For example, having collected data on all the symptoms there was the problem of grouping them into different diseases. It was therefore important to devise problem-formation heuristics that can partition sets of disease hypotheses evoked by the clinical data. This was accomplished with the successor, INTERNIST-II or CADUCEUS, which was designed with a system for partitioning disease hypotheses into coherent sub-sets.

The uniqueness of INTERNIST-I and its successors is that they simulate the actual techniques of a clinician. Schaffner (1985, p.19) suggests that the diagnostic powers of INTERNIST-I is qualitatively similar to that of hospital clinicians but inferior to that of expert case discussants. But as Polanyi (1958) has argued in another context, many of the discovery techniques employed by scientists (and the same point applies to diagnosticians) are based on forms of tacit knowledge which is not expressed in the manuals and textbooks related to the discipline in question. For the the philosophy of science the extent to which these aspects of tacit knowledge can be incorporated into a computer program is one of the most challenging and fascinating aspects of INTERNIST-I and CADUCEUS. (McMullin, 1985)

INTERNIST-I operates according to the following stages.

1.   The generative stage

The system is first provided with information about a patient in the form of manifestations of the disease. The program then generates disease hypotheses that may account for the manifestations. This is a simple triggering process that employs lists of data which link the manifestations to various diseases. These hypotheses are then ranked according to evaluative scores reflecting their fit with the data. Credit is given to hypotheses which have the highest score of manifestations. Counting against a specific disease will be manifestations expected, but not present in this particular patient's case, and manifestations not accounted for by the disease hypothesis. (Schaffner, 1985, p.16)

2.   *Preliminary evaluation and rule out*

Having attributed evaluative scores to the disease hypothesis the top ranking ones (above a certain threshold) are then sorted out as competitors. If the leading disease hypothesis has ninety points higher than its nearest competitor, the program can conclude with a diagnosis. If not the program goes into one of its searching modes which assesses the competitors according to a point scale. At this stage further information may be sought in order to rank the various competing hypotheses and to rule out the less plausible ones.

3.   *Strong evaluation or pursuit*

If no conclusive diagnosis has been reached in the first two stages then the topmost hypotheses will be subjected to the pursue mode, which asks specific questions related to the hypothesis. This phase has been described as 'strong evaluation'. (Schaffner, 1980) If a sufficiently high level of points have not been attained, and other competitors remain fairly close, then the program reverts to a rule out mode to reduce the number of competitors. If this leaves two to four competitors fairly close to the leading hypothesis then the program enters its discriminate mode, where further questions are designed to increase the separation of scores between the competing hypotheses. At this stage questions will be put forward in order to either support one hypothesis or downgrade another. Finally, when a leading contender emerges - if one is deemed strong enough - a pursue mode comes into effect to confirm that diagnosis. Once the first diagnosis is concluded the program recycles in order to explain the remaining unexplained manifestations of the disease, and make additional diagnoses where evidence is inadequate.

Of course, the program need not always terminate with a diagnosis. If all the questions have been asked and no conclusion is reached, then the program will 'defer' and terminate with the remaining competitors ranked in descending order.

Thus described, INTERNIST-I, and its successors, conform to Schaffner's formulation of the requirements for a logic of discovery, as the process involves 1) a generative phase, where the signs evoke disease models; 2) a preliminary evaluative phase, where disease models are weighted, and 3) a strong evaluative phase in which models are eliminated and a conclusion reached.

A Logic of Prior Assessment

The case for a logic of generation was reinforced by Martin Curd (1980, p.202) who defined a 'period of theory generation' as a process beginning when a scientist or research group first begin thinking seriously about a problem and ending when the theory is written down in a form suitable for publication'. During this time the theory will not have been experimentally tested, that is, no result 'not necessarily known' will have been derived from it. (ibid, p.202) For example: 'In the case of the discovery of the double-helix model of DNA, the period of theory generation began with the first collaboration of Watson and Crick on the problem in 1951 and ended with the appearance of their famous paper in the journal Nature in 1953'. (ibid, p202) According to Curd the period of theory generation must contain a logic of prior assessment which involves the methodological appraisal of hypotheses after they have been generated but before they have been tested. This is in line with Newell, Simon, and Schaffner's respective heuristic guidelines for the reduction of hypotheses. For in a period of theory generation a limit has to be set upon the flood of hypotheses which can be derived from a finite body of empirical data.

There are two types of prior assessment, which can be depicted as 1) a logic of probability, and 2) a logic of pursuit. Whilst the former is bound up with what a scientist or group of scientists believe to be what is probably true, the latter is concerned with questions like 'What shall we jetison?' 'What shall we rule out?' and 'What shall we continue with?' For Curd (ibid, p.205) it is the logic of pursuit which is of interest to the scientist and is the 'real key' to the logic of discovery. Reasons in the logic of pursuit may be pragmatic, or derived from criteria for simplicity. These need not provide necessary and sufficient grounds for determining the truth of a theory; they indicate a preference for theories that are easier to work with. Curd (ibid, p.214) stresses the pragmatic nature of assessment in the logic of pursuit.

> We pursue explanatory theories because they are the kinds of theory we are interested in having. Explanitoriness is a stipulative requirement on our part, not necessarily a reliable indicator of truth. Simplicity is not necessarily a sign that we have unlocked the mysteries of nature but a prudent preference for theories that are easy to work with and to test.

The pragmatic nature of the reasons employed in the logic of pursuit allow for a wide range of pursuable options. Simplicity, cost, implications for the environment, military applications, and potential side effects which may yield financial rewards, may all be employed to justify further pursuit. A logic of pursuit provides only *prima facie* grounds for adhering to an hypothesis, but such a logic indicates the rationality of discovery.

If Schaffner and Curd are correct, there is no qualitative distinction between the context of discovery and the context of justification. Reasons are appropriate in both the preliminary stages of discovery as well as in later stages. The only difference is that 'in the context of justification...the substantive evidence will be systematically organised, often further developed, and will in general be more powerful'. (Schaffner, 1980, p.191) By 'more powerful' it is implied that there will be more coherence and greater empirical adequacy. But a logic of discovery - if it is to avoid collapsing into the H-D model - must acknowledge a logic of generation. Schaffner and Curd's respective accounts of discovery draw attention to the importance of a logic of generation and a logic of preliminary evaluation. It can also be said that actual discoveries involve both of these aspects. Unfortunately recollections of the generative phase are too often couched in terms of dramatic 'illuminations' and irrationalist flights of distraction.

Having established the basis for a logic of discovery which recognises the interplay between a logic of generation and a logic of evaluation what now remains is to characterise the process of discovery in terms of various stages, each of which can be subjected to rational assessment.

VI Preliminary evaluation, pursuit, rule out and adoption

Preliminary Evaluation and Pursuit

While the task of the generator is to provide and regulate new solutions and hypotheses, the function of preliminary evaluation is to cull the implausible. Once an idea, tentative solution to a problem or a hypothesis, has been generated it can be subjected to various forms of preliminary evaluation. A hypothesis may be deemed initially plausible, then pursued, but ruled out during preliminary evaluation. This appears to have been the fate of many initially plausible hypotheses, ranging from Galileo's explanation of tidal motion in terms of the double motion of the Earth, to Freud's initial confusion between dreams and latent dream thoughts.

The concepts of preliminary evaluation, pursuit and rule out are necessarily bound up with each other. A proposal is pursued during preliminary evaluation pending rule out. Subsequently, stronger evaluation may be required with appropriate modes of further pursuit and rule out. An example from popular detective fiction illustrates these essential features. The fact that the butler's fingerprints are on the gun which was found near the body in the library may serve as an initially plausible explanation as to who committed the murder and as to why the butler has disappeared. There are good reasons for suggesting and pursuing the hypothesis that the butler is the culprit. But these reasons are neither necessary nor sufficient. He may not have committed the murder but unwittingly handled the gun, then left suddenly assuming that as it was known that he harboured ill feelings towards the victim he would be the prime suspect. On further investigation of this explanation together with knowledge of the butler's character and other facts regarding his whereabouts at the precise time of the murder, the detective rules out the butler hypothesis and pursues an alternative but initially plausible suggestion that the deceased's nephew, as sole beneficiary to the estate, had good reasons to commit the crime. This hypothesis may then be pursued until it too is either ruled out, or subjected to stronger evaluation and further pursuit, or finally adopted.

In the context of preliminary evaluation the constraints may be somewhat tighter than in the generative stage, yet they may be significantly looser than required for later adoption. Laudan (1980) comes very close to this position when he argues for the recognition of a middle stage between the context of discovery and justification, thus replacing the two-context distinction with a trichotomy. Says Laudan (1980, p.174): 'Between the context of discovery and the context of ultimate justification, there is a nether region, which I have called the *context of pursuit*'. This threefold distinction is presented as an improvement over the traditional version for the following reasons:

> These contexts mark the temporal, not the logical, history of a concept. It is first discovered; if found worthy of pursuit, it is entertained; if further evaluation shows it to be worthy of belief, it is accepted. More importantly this trichotomy prevents us from lumping together activities and modalities of appraisal which have frequently but erroneously been confused with one another. (ibid, p.174)

There are two reservations with Laudan's account. First, merely adding another context to the two-context distinction leaves the generative stage as an irrational moment. Second, although a pursuit phase is an important stage between the generation and adoption of hypotheses, Laudan's trichotomy does not capture the idea of discovery as a process. In fact Laudan sees the context of discovery in traditional terms, as an irrational event. Thus he speaks of discovery in terms of 'the "*eureka*" moment", i.e., the time when a new idea or conception first dawns'. He also shares with Popper, and other exponents of the two-context theory, the view that it is not the task of philosophers to investigate the genesis of theories. (ibid, p.182)

Laudan's trichotomy, if accepted, would be damaging to attempts to portray a logic of discovery. For Laudan the creative process is unanalysable and the abductive methods of Peirce and Hanson belong only to the context of pursuit. Contrasting contemporary approaches to the logic of discovery with the older foundationalist or infallibilist methods, Laudan maintains that the reasoning processes in the context of discovery have no epistemic value. 'The older programme for a logic of discovery', he says, 'was addressed to the unquestionably important philosophical problem of providing an epistemic warrant for accepting scientific theories. The newer programme for a logic of discovery, by contrast, has yet to make clear what philosophical problems about science it is addressing. (ibid, p.182)

But Laudan and others who challenge the 'friends of discovery' do so from within the standpoint of the old dichotomy between discovery and justification, according to which there is a temporal gap between the two (or on Laudan's terms three) contexts such that propositions advanced in each can be independently classified. Laudan's challenge to the 'friends of discovery' will not be met with attempts to demonstrate the epistemic status of the context of discovery, but by challenging the very idea of sharply delineated contexts, whether temporal or logical. It is not that there are two, or three, contexts where one or more have greater epistemic status or where one precedes the others in any temporal sequence, but that discovery is a process wherein generation, evaluation, pursuit, tests and further hypothesising may occur in any order. It might even be argued that the dichotomising categories with which philosophers have caricatured discovery actually stand in the way of an effective logical appraisal of the sciences.

For Laudan there is a neat sequence from the context of discovery to pursuit and finally 'ultimate justification'. To break the hold of this model and conceptualise discovery as a process it will help if the expressions 'context of discovery' and 'context of justification' are replaced with a series of expressions which might include 'initial thinking', 'preliminary evaluation', 'pursuit', 'rule out', and 'adoption', any of which can be interchangeable in either a logical or temporal sense. If seen as a process, discovery would have an indefinite number of intermediate stages.

Some useful expressions might be 'initial thinking', which refers to the generation of initially plausible ideas. Then 'preliminary evaluation', where less plausible ideas are ruled out whilst more favourable ones are pursued until they are either themselves ruled out or adopted. Among the criteria for pursuit may be some set of properties by means of which a theory is deemed to be worth entertaining. For Rachael Laudan (1987, p.204) this would reflect 'the willingness of scientists (or the scientific community) to admit a new theory to a group of theories worthy of consideration'. The pursuit of an entertaining hypothesis operates within rational restraints. The imaginative possibilities of brains in a vat or life on Alpha Centauri, or any other fictional possibilities envisaged by philosophers, might not be worthy of pursuit. A hypothesis that is envisaged, but unlikely to be pursued, is of no value. In science only envisaged pursuable hypotheses are relevant. If a theory is entertaining it can be the subject of a mode of pursuit which might involve its further development 'whether by articulating its theoretical base or by collecting evidence for its appraisal' (ibid, p.204). It may at some stage undergo stronger pursuit, further pursuit, and so on, according to the complexity of its subject matter and the number of plausible alternatives.

Aesthetic Considerations

Aesthetic considerations play an influential role in the various stages of preliminary evaluation. For some, aesthetic considerations are the very paradigm of irrationality and consequently a sharp distinction is advocated between aesthetic considerations in the context of discovery and rational judgements in the logic of justification. Even those who endorse aesthetic considerations in science have either implicitly or explicitly seen them as extraneous features unamenable to rational assessment. Polanyi (1981) was actually misleading when he said that 'intuitions of coherence' were subjective 'emotional qualities'. Coherence and simplicity are not merely emotional qualities; the recognition of these aspects has proved too often to be scientifically beneficial. Part of the legacy of logical empiricism is the tendency to lump aesthetic judgements, together with ethical and religious judgements, under the headings 'emotional' and ' subjective'. Within recent years aestheticians, ethicists and philosophers of religion, have demonstrated the wrongheadedness of this approach. In aesthetics, ethics and religion, one can provide objective judgements and clearly distinguish them from emotional responses. But the reluctance to accept aesthetic judgements as candidates for scientific reasoning is still very powerful. In many cases a scientist may have good reasons to employ aesthetic judgements. That heliocentrism was theoretically simpler and technically easier to manage than the hypothesis of a geocentric universe was an aesthetic fact which gave Copernicus and others good reasons for putting forward the heliocentric hypothesis. Admittedly, in this case, it was not a sufficient reason, but it was a very good reason, worth entertaining and pursuing.

There are good old fashioned inductive reasons for treating the simplicity of a theory as grounds for entertainment and pursuit. In many cases the simplest formulation has turned out to be the correct one. Thus, says Wesley C. Salmon (1970, p.86), when Watson and Crick 'were enraptured by the beauty of the double-helix hypothesis, I believe that their reaction was more than purely aesthetic. Experience indicates that hypotheses of that degree of simplicity tend to be successful, and that they were inferring that it had not only beauty, but a good chance of being correct'. In cases of this kind there are good reasons for aesthetic considerations because the aesthetic judgement is made against the background of scientific experience concerning the kinds of hypotheses which work well scientifically.

Familiarity with successful hypotheses is an important regulative feature of scientific discovery which philosophers ignore at their peril when making rational assessments of creative work. The plausibility of a scientific hypothesis is often established with reference to past experience in dealing with other scientific hypotheses of a similar type. This is another important feature of Simon's appeal to pattern discovery processes; we can, if we are sufficiently well informed, recognise the patterns of successful work. Hence Darwin's theory of natural selection was plausible, even in its initial stages, because success had been associated with similar theories in geology. On the other hand a low plausibility rating would be given to hypotheses which conflict with established successes, despite the fact that they may, on occasions, turn out to be correct.

The appeal of simplicity is bound up with a feature known as consilience. A theory is consilient if it has the ability to unify many distinct classes of facts. Darwinian theory was ultimately superior to many of its rivals because it explained diverse classes of facts, such as the geographical distribution of species, and the existence of rudimentary organs. But breadth of explanation is of little value without criteria for simplicity, as the most consilient theory in any problem field, which could explain everything, would probably turn out to be the most unwieldy one. Simplicity puts a constraint on consilience: a theory is simpler if it requires fewer special assumptions than its competitors. (Holland et al, 1986, p,334) For example, Creationism explains many diverse facts and might even be more consilient than Darwinism. It explains the characteristics of any species, given the assumption that God willed them. But it lacks simplicity in that it requires an assumption for every fact explained. It requires an assumption to explain the fact that elephants have trunks and humans have two eyes. But, if necessary, other special assumptions could equally explain why the elephant had two trunks or humans had had three eyes.

It is very hard to exclude aesthetic considerations from scientific practice. Not only was Copernicus initially attracted to heliocentrism for its simplicity and consilience but the same reasons supported the rule out of alternatives. Simplicity also indicated that it might be a truer theory than its rivals. The force of simplicity is no less strong in the twentieth century, particularly in the work of Einstein.

Einstein's General Theory of Relativity was deemed initially plausible and worth entertaining largely on aesthetic grounds whilst observations of its predictions played a very secondary role in this context. The power of aesthetic considerations in Einstein's work has been examined by S. Chandrasekhar (1987, p.166) who refers to the following statement by Einstein on the announcement of his field-equations in November 1915: 'Anyone who fully comprehends this theory cannot escape its magic'. This 'magic' or aesthetic appeal exerted priority over factual confirmation. Despite widespread endorsement confirming instances of the General Theory have not been prolific. And whilst successful verifications of the lowest first order departures from Newtonian theory have lent support to the General Theory, they have so far only related to 'departures from the predictions of the Newtonian theory by a few parts in a million, and of no more than three or four parameters in a post-Newtonian expansion of the Einstein field-equations'. (ibid, p.148) Moreover, 'no predictions of General Relativity, in the limit of strong gravitational fields, have received any confirmation; and none seems likely in the foreseeable future'. (ibid, p.148) Any theory which supersedes such a well established one as Newtonian theory should normally refer to predictions which relate to major aspects, rather than small order departures. Chandrasekhar asks whether other theories would have been so readily accepted had they only predicted small order departures from the theories they displaced. Would Dirac's theory of the electron have been accepted without 'the discovery, in accordance with the theory, of electron-positron pairs in cosmic ray showers?' (ibid, p.149) 'Would our faith in Maxwell's equations of electromagnetic field be as universal as it is without Hertz's experiments on the propogation of electromagnetic waves with precisely the same velocity of light *and* without Poincaré's proof of their invariance to Lorentz's transformations?' (ibid, p.149)

One might argue that the occurrence of black holes confirm predictions derived from the theory, but Chandrasekhar objects: 'The notion that light cannot escape from a sufficiently strong gravitational field is an inference not based on any exact prediction of a theory; it depends only on the empirical fact that light is affected by gravity'. (ibid, p.149)

In the absence of any major refutations of Newtonian theory and confirming instances of the General Theory, Chandrasekhar concludes that 'faith and confidence' in the General Theory of Relativity is derived from aesthetic sources, from the 'beauty of the mathematical description of Nature that the theory provides'. (ibid, p.150) But the force of aesthetics in Einstein's theories was not merely the appeal of some intrinsic quality of beauty or subjective emotional response to it; it was bound up with principles of internal consistency and on 'its freedom from contradiction with parts of physics not contemplated in the formulation of the theory'. (ibid, p.150) The General Theory of Relativity is not only internally consistent, it is also consistent with 'the entire domain of physics outside the realm originally contemplated'. (ibid, p.150) For example, the notion of entropy derived from the theory is compatible with the laws of thermodynamics and statistical mechanics, and the theory does not violate Newtonian theory or is violated by quantum theory. (Röhrlich, 1987)

Yet even the consistency requirement is only part of a much deeper principle; a metaphysical demand for the ultimate unification of reality, which Einstein (1939, pp.139-140) expressed some time after publication of the General Theory.

> Behind the tireless efforts of the investigator there lurks a stronger, more mysterious desire: it is existence and reality that one wishes to comprehend...we are seeking for the simplest possible system of thought which will bind together the observed facts...the special aim which I have constantly before me is logical unification in the field of physics.

In contemporary physics there is a mystical aesthetic attitude which Kepler would approve of; the reliance upon abstract principles of symmetry goes hand in hand with rigorous experimental work. Although it is clear that scientists may be guided by aesthetic considerations, it is too frequently assumed that these considerations are only relevant in the description of theories, not in their genesis and pursuit. In a letter to Einstein, Werner Heisenberg (1971, p.68) expressed fears that aesthetic considerations would detract from the rigour of his work. Yet as the following remarks indicate, intellectual honesty requires recognition of the power of simplicity and beauty.

> You may object that by speaking of simplicity and beauty I am introducing aesthetic criteria of truth, and I frankly admit that I am strongly attracted by the simplicity and beauty of the mathematical schemes which nature presents us. You must have felt this too: the almost frightening simplicity and wholeness of the relationship, which nature suddenly spreads out before us...

Simplicity is no guarantee of success, and concern with simple explanations may inhibit progress. It took Kepler ten years to retreat from the simplicity of a circle to the complexity of an ellipse. There is also a degree of tension between aesthetic considerations and the practical consequences of scientific theories, which can be seen in the two main theories of twentieth-century physics: General Relativity Theory and Quantum Theory. Einstein's General Theory of Relativity is founded on very clear and elegant principles; it is fundamentally simple, mathematically attractive, and reduces gravity to geometry. It is both philosophically and aesthetically attractive. In contrast, Quantum Theory has less aesthetic appeal. Its founding postulates are counterintuitive, and its philosophical inconsistencies have been the source of much criticism. Yet its successful applications exceed those of General Relativity Theory. Quantum mechanics is now considered to be 'an indispensible part of particle physics, nuclear, atomic, molecular and solid state physics, physical chemistry, modern optics, stellar astrophysics and cosmology'. (Davies and Brown, 1988, p.52)

Rule Out and Falsification

The rule out mode, which is a feature of preliminary evaluation, is compatible with criteria for falsification. But it must be stressed that rule out, unlike falsification, is not linked to criteria for demarcation between science and pseudo-science: it simply indicates an important stage in the development of a scientific hypothesis.

Popper's theory of demarcation has generated one of the most heated discussions in the philosophy of science. According to Popper a research programme can be hailed as a piece of genuine scientific work if its hypotheses yield propositions which can, in principle, be falsified. Programmes which do not yield falsifiable predictions are deemed to be unscientific. Freudian psycho-analysis is presented by Popper as an example of pseudo- science, since its explanatory hypotheses are not, it is alleged, potentially falsifiable. Thus if a Freudian suggests that paranoid patients have strong homosexual desires, the very denial of these desires might be cited as evidence of a subconscious strategy, known as 'reaction formation', for concealing their existence. The Freudian would seem to be in a no lose situation; whatever the patient's response, the initial diagnosis is correct. But this strength, argues Popper, is only apparent because lack of potential falsification robs the theory of all rigour and disqualifies it as a respectable branch of science.

The extent to which this view rests on a caricature of Freud has been examined elsewhere (Grünbaum, 1979) and is not at issue here. Furthermore H.J. Eysenck and others have made numerous claims, based on carefully conducted experiments, to have decisively refuted the main aspects of Freudian theory. Thus if it is possible to refute, or at least claim to have refuted, Freudian theory, then the theory cannot be unscientific on Popper's terms.

Nevertheless, a proper understanding of rule out - although it will not show Freud to have been unscientific - might reveal certain inherent weaknesses in some aspects of his theories and explain why there are grounds for scepticism.

It is partly the failure to rule out plausible rival hypotheses that ultimately weakens Freudian experimental claims rather than any alleged dogmatic resistance to falsification. In an assessment of the status of experimental studies - of which there are now over 1,000 - purporting to test Freudian hypotheses Edward Erwin (1988) indicates that the key weakness of Freudian theory is its failure to rule out plausible alternatives. According to Erwin (ibid, pp.128-9): 'If a Freudian hypothesis H^1, has an incompatible rival H^2, that explains the data just as well, and is of equal or greater plausibility all things considered, then we are not warranted in believing the Freudian hypothesis on the basis of experimental evidence. It could be argued that some small degree of confirmation is provided for both H^1 and H^2, but the confirmation, if it exists at all, cannot be of a strong kind'. That is to say, if we know that H^1 and H^2 are incompatible then we are not obliged to adopt either one.

A central issue here is Freud's hypothesis that paranoid males are characterised by strong homosexual desires. In one experiment reported by Erwin paranoid subjects, when offered a preference of either male or female pictures, looked longer at the male photographs when the purpose of the task was disguised. (They were asked to determine which figure in each picture was the larger.) This observation could thus be presented as corroboration of Freud's theory. But when asked for an explicit preference they stated a preference for the photographs of women. This observation could then be seen as a corroboration of Freud's theory of reaction formation. It would seem that either observation adds weight to the Freudian explanation.

However, there are several other plausible explanations of the subject's preferences. One is that, being generally suspicious they found the males more of a threat, hence they looked at them longer. As for the stated preferences for photographs of women, a plausible explanation might be that they truly preferred to look at pictures of females. Both of these hypotheses are plausible rivals to the Freudian explanation, which are not ruled out, but simply ignored.

According to Popper, Marxism is also a paradigm of pseudo science: it allegedly provides explanations, but any predictions derived from them fail to meet the criterion of falsifiability. However, if Marxism is viewed from the standpoint of a logic of discovery its main theories are entirely compatible with criteria for a logic of generation and preliminary evaluation. The logic of Marx's theories is generative in the sense that the method is largely one of hypothesis formation regulated by certain theories and values. What Marxism does is provide highly plausible accounts of the mechanisms that must exist in order to account for the structure and dynamics of capitalist society. Marxism postulates the existence of certain relations and underlying causes which, if they exist, can be cited in the evaluation and elimination of several alternative explanations of social phenomena. In this sense some of Marx's hypotheses, such as the law of capitalist development, can be said to conform to a logic of generation and preliminary evaluation. Likewise, his postulation of the existence of social classes generates explanations of social change and the dynamics of history.

The significance of preliminary evaluation, pursuit and a rule out phase is that they cover those periods when scientists may have generated several plausible hypotheses, but only wish to pursue one or two of them further. This can be illustrated with some familiar examples from the history of science.

The Discovery of Uranus

On the night of March 13th. 1781, the astronomer William Herschell recorded in his journal, after observing the northern heavens, that he had seen either a nebulous star or a comet in 'the quartile near Zeta Tauri'. This entry is said to record the discovery of the planet Uranus. Yet between 1690 and 1781 the same object had been recorded at least 17 times by astronomers who had classified it as a star. (Kuhn, 1977, p.171) Given the nature of the problem only three plausible explanations of the phenomenon could be generated out of the observations. It had to be either 1) a star, 2) a comet, or 3) a planet. Further candidates could not be entertained for the structure of the problem itself defined the scope of plausible solutions. Despite advocacy of an unlimited proliferation of hypotheses in the context of discovery it is quite obvious that such a course would involve instant loss of credibility. Having initially generated three rational explanations a preliminary evaluation could determine which could be ruled out and which could be pursued. Since Herschell had access to a 'superior technique' for making observations - a telescope with much greater magnification than any of his contemporaries had access to - the observed nearness of the object enabled him to rule out the star hypothesis. It was much to near to be a star. However, the large appearance of the object left it plausible to pursue the suggestion that it might either be a comet or a planet. He published an announcement that he had observed a comet, noting, however, that it was unusual because it did not have a tail.

The comet conjecture was given a degree of support by two observations on the 17 and 19 March, 1781, which indicated that the object moved among the stars. As a result astronomers all over Europe were informed of the discovery of a new comet and mathematicians began to compute its path. But within a month this explanation had to be ruled out. Its orbit was not like a comet and could not be predicted on this basis. Repeated observations failed to confirm the comet conjecture. Nevil Maskelyne, the English Astronomer Royal, was first to suspect that the new object was not a comet. Herschell's friend, Dr William Watson, suggested to him that it might be a planet. (Littman, 1989, pp.5-6) Mathematical proof came in the summer of 1781 from the Swedish astronomer, Anders Johan Lexell. Further computations were made, using a planet's rather than a comet's orbit. By 1783 Simon Laplace and Francois Andre) Mechain had calculated its elliptical orbit, although for some time astronomers had acknowledged that the object was a planet which had been named Uranus some six months after Herschell's first observations.

Figure I

Problem	New phenomenon observed in the heavens. What is it?
	Initial Thinking
Solution 1	A star
Solution 2	A comet
Solution 3	A planet
	Preliminary Evaluation, Pursuit and Rule Out
Solution 1	Rule out, since superior observational techniques indicate that its too near to be a star.
Solution 2	Pursue and calculate its orbit. Rule out, since observations fail

	to secure that the orbit is that of a comet.
Solution 3	Pursue and calculate its orbit. If planetary orbit is confirmed then adopt solution 3.

The Discovery of Neptune

The calculations worked out in 1783 demonstrated that Uranus followed a planetary orbit, but there was still considerable difficulty in formulating precise predictions of its orbit. More calculations were made throughout the first half of the nineteenth century but they all failed to account for Uranus' seemingly wayward behaviour. Several wild hypotheses were introduced, including the suggestion that Uranus had been knocked off course by a comet. It was widely held that the failure to explain the aberrations in Uranus' orbit amounted to a scandal in nineteenth-century astronomy. The observed orbit was clearly incompatible with predictions made on the basis of established Newtonian theory. Uranus appeared to be defying the law of gravity. At the level of initial thinking at least three plausible solutions to the problem could be generated. First, Newtonian theory had been decisively falsified. The consequence being that an alternative theory of motion would have to replace it. One alternative that was actually proposed entailed the revival of the Cartesian idea of a cosmic fluid with vortices filled with space between heavenly bodies. Insufficient evidence for the existence of this fluid killed off this suggestion. (Littman, 1989, p.27) Second, it was suggested that the range of Newtonian theory would have to be limited; that is, the inverse square law would have to be restricted. It was suggested that Newtonian theory works satisfactorily up to a distance short of Uranus. Beyond that the behaviour of the outer planets would have to be explained by means of another law. With mathematical ingenuity a new law could have been developed in order to account for Uranus' irregularities. Such an ad hoc solution could merit a high plausibility rating, for in many branches of science anomalies are cordoned off to prevent outright dismissal of the theory or programme as a whole. The third possibility was to postulate the existence of an undiscovered planet with enough gravitational force to explain Uranus' irregular orbit.

On further examination the three solutions to the problem do not merit equal weighting. The first two can be shown to have less plausibility than the latter, for the rejection or dramatic modification of a highly successful heuristic is a step which a scientific community is reluctant to take. The anomaly merely spurred serious scientists to provide an explanation within the framework of Newtonian theory. Only those with a very superficial knowledge of Newtonian theory would be inclined to reject the entire theory. In this respect Imre Lakatos (1970) is entirely correct to insist that there can be no falsification of a research programme without another to replace it.

The third option was pursued, and by the end of the 1830's most astronomers believed that an unseen planet lay beyond Uranus. In 1845 the English mathematician, John Couch Adams, calculated the position of the new body affecting Uranus. By 1846 the Frenchman, Urbain Jean Joseph Leverrier had independently calculated its position. Both men had reasoned to the hypothesis of an outer planet from within the standpoint of Newtonian mechanics by calculating the mass and location of a body capable of effecting the known aberrations in the orbit of the planet Uranus. On the night of September 24, 1846, the new planet was observed by Johann Gottfried Galle at the Berlin Observatory, and the Neptune solution was adopted.

Figure II

Problem	Explain aberrations in Uranus's orbit. The background knowledge indicates that this is anomaly within classical mechanics, between the predictions made on the basis of Newtonian theory and reliable observations to the contrary.
	Initial Thinking
Solution 1	Newton's theory of Universal Gravitation has been falsified.
Solution 2	The range of Newton's theory must be restricted.

Solution 3	Postulate mass to explain gravitational action on Uranus.
	Preliminary Evaluation, Pursuit and Rule Out.
Solution 1	Seek alternative theory to Newton's. Note that this objective would entail major changes in existing theories.
Solution 2	Postulate modifications to Newton's theory in order to cordon off the anomaly. Note that this would entail major changes in existing theories.
Solution 3	Calculate mass of hypothetised planet and calculate its location. Continue in pursuit mode pending empirical confirmation of predictions. If the planet is observed rule out solutions 1 and 2.

The Non-Discovery of Vulcan

The discovery of Neptune through the calculations of Adams and Leverrier proved to be one of the high points of Newtonian theory. The same retroductive approach was applied to explain the superficially similar aberrations in the perihelion of the planet Mercury, a phenomenon discovered by Leverrier. Mercury's perihelion was 'advancing along its orbit at a rate of about nine minutes twenty six seconds a century - less than one third the apparent diameter of the Moon as seen from Earth'. (Littman, 1989, p.58) Leverrier explained Mercury's problems by means of an initially plausible prediction of an intra-Mercurian planet which he called Vulcan. This, for Leverrier, was a plausible hypothesis but it then had to undergo preliminary evaluation. Unlike the prediction of Neptune, which was observed within weeks of Leverrier's published calculations, Vulcan remained unobservable. There were, however, several astronomers who claimed to have observed Vulcan but all were discredited. Nevertheless each claim reinforced the entertainment value of the search.

These features which made the Vulcan hypothesis worth entertaining, delayed rule out for as long as it remained plausible to maintain that the planet was either always obscured by the rays of the sun or that it was an incredibly dense body of small dimensions - too small for existing instruments to detect - or that it was a cloud of asteroids. All of these considerations can be rationally generated from Leverrier's background knowledge. However, if the initial hypothesis was to survive the stages of preliminary evaluation and be adopted, then Vulcan, like Neptune, would have to be there. Moreover, the explanations of Vulcan's inobservability would also have to survive further evaluation and rule out. But on further investigation one of Leverrier's explanations of Vulcan's inobservability entailed a commitment to the improbable and patently false belief that the positions of the Sun, the Earth, and Vulcan, constituted a permanent straight line. Moreover, if (according to another one of Leverrier's hypotheses) Vulcan shared the Earth's period of revolution in order to remain permanently behind the Sun, then this too would invalidate Kepler's Third Law, $T^2 = r^3$. (Hanson, 1963, 1971) On these terms the range of plausible inferences generated in support of the Vulcan hypothesis would be regulated by their incompatibility with other known data.

If the Neptune and Vulcan hypotheses are compared, Leverrier's retroductive reasoning is eminently successful in the first instance but the hypotheses he generated in the latter failed in the pursue mode. This failure initiated a destabilisation of the classical mechanics of Newton and Laplace. But as the existant theory was to remain capable of generating solutions to other problems classical mechanics was not modified until Einstein published his General Theory of Relativity in 1916 from which Mercury's perihelial advance could be explained. As long as no alternative theory was available astronomers were able to persist with their existing, though imperfect, concepts. To have abandoned them prematurely would have meant the rejection of science and rational thought.

Figure III

Problem   Explain aberrations in Mercury's
                                     perihelion.
                                     The background knowledge
                                     indicates that this is an anomaly
                                     within the terms of classical
                                     mechanics, between the predictions
                                     made on the basis of Newtonian
                                     theory and reliable observations to
                                     the contrary.

	Initial Thinking
Solution 1	From analogy with the solution to the problem of Uranus's orbit postulate mass of sufficient dimensions to account for Mercury's orbit. Predict existence of the planet Vulcan.
	Preliminary Evaluation, Pursuit and Rule Out
Solution 1	Calculate mass and location of Vulcan. Continue in pursuit mode pending empirical confirmation.
Problem	No observations available to confirm the existence of any intra Mercurian planet.
Solution 1	Vulcan is hidden by the Sun.
Solution 2	Vulcan is too small to be detected by conventional means.
Solution 3	Postulated mass is not a planet, but a cloud of asteroids.
	Preliminary Evaluation, Pursuit, and Rule Out
Solutions 1,2,3.	Rule out, as they entail predictions wildly incompatible with known positions of the Sun and other well founded data.

No satisfactory solution. Return to generative mode and/or consider redefinition of the problem.

The discovery of Neptune in 1846 was hailed as a solution to the problem of the aberrations in Uranus's orbit, although small discrepancies remained. Both the major outer planets, Neptune and Uranus, appeared to move around their orbits at an uneven rate. This could be explained in terms of slight errors in the measurements and calculations, but then it could be due to the influence of another planet. The difficulties in calculating and observing a trans-Neptunian planet were too formidable for most nineteenth-century astronomers and the problem was shelved. At the outset of the twentieth century a firm conviction regarding a trans-Neptunian planet was held by two American astronomers, Percival Lowell and William H. Pickering. Both men attempted to predict the location of the planet which was later called Pluto, and their results were not that dissimilar. Although Pickering came as close as Lowell in predicting the location of Pluto, the rate at which he generated and modified his predictions cast doubt upon his scientific credibility. Convinced that the mass of the as yet unseen planet was 6.7 times that of the Earth, Lowell began an earnest search in 1905 by means of a photographic survey along the mean plane of the solar system. This proved unsatisfactory. After many more years of searching, using a variety of techniques, in 1915 he gave up the search for what he had named 'Planet X'. He died in 1916 unaware that his predicted location of the trans-Neptunian planet - too small for detection with his nine inch telescope - was almost correct.

In 1929 the search was taken up at the Lowell Observatory by Clyde Tombaugh who, working with a thirteen inch refractor, finally located Pluto on February 18th, 1930, two thirds of a degree east of the star, Delta Geminorum. In the following years new telescopes and techniques were to reveal that the size of Pluto was much smaller than it was originally held; that it was several thousands less than the size of the Earth. Being considerably smaller than the Moon it is therefore unlikely to possess the necessary density (which would have to be many more times that of lead) and it has been ruled out as an explanation of the peturbations of the outer planets.

Problems continue to unsettle astronomers with regard to the calculations for the orbits of Uranus and Neptune. Their orbital periods have not been satisfactorily observed. Uranus takes 84 years to orbit the Sun, which means that it has only completed two and a half orbits since its discovery in 1781, whilst Neptune has yet to have been observed completing its full orbit of 165 years since its discovery in 1846. So far none of the data on either planet fits any of the predicted orbits and considerable doubt has been cast upon the calculations of nineteenth-century astronomers.

During the 1980's several astronomers became increasingly convinced of the existence of a tenth planet in the Solar System whose mass is capable of influencing the orbits of the outer planets. For some time evidence had been gathered concerning the gravitational influence of a large mass at the outer edge of the Solar System. The most active astronomers in pursuit of the tenth planet have been Thomas C. van Flandern and Robert S. Harrington, Daniel P. Whitmire and John J. Matese, John D. Anderson, and Conley Powell. (Littman, 1989, p.197) The name 'Humphrey' was suggested as a possible name for Planet 10 by Robert S. Harrington of the U.S. Naval Observatory.

In the initial stages of the inquiry several alternative hypotheses to the tenth planet were plausible, but by 1987 they were ruled out. One suggestion involved the prediction of a possible stellar companion to the Sun (a dim star orbiting the Sun) but much further out than any of the planets. Another suggestion was that a cluster of asteroids or comets lay somewhere beyond Neptune. But these hypotheses were excluded when Pioneer 10 was tracked after passing beyond Pluto, and showed no evidence of gravitational effects that would support the existence of such phenomena.

But the problem of explaining the peturbations in the orbits of Uranus and Neptune remained. For this reason the Planet 10 hypothesis was given further pursuit. In 1979 Harrington began a search using brute force methods, supplying a computer with thousands of orbits and ruling out the impossible ones. He continued his search in 1980 using a 24 inch telescope, and then again throughout the 1980's using other equipment, with no success. New checks on the data were completed in 1987 by John Anderson of NASA's Jet Propulsion Laboratories. Anderson monitered the space probes, Pioneers 10 and 11, which were launched in 1972. By 1987 Pioneer 10 was well beyond Pluto. The evidence from the Pioneer probes was vastly superior to previous methods of obtaining evidence of planetary motion because space probes emit radio signals at a precise frequency, which allows detection of even slight accelerations by a change of frequency. But the space probes did not appear to have made contact with any unusual gravitational force.

Ironically, Anderson held that this very lack of evidence from the spacecraft could actually be interpreted as evidence in favour of the new planet. According to well-founded sources Uranus and Neptune have only been observed to have been affected for a limited period - between 1810 and 1910. Since 1910 there has been no signs of disturbance. This would suggest that the tenth planet follows a highly elliptical orbit that has carried it too far away for it too have any significant effect on Uranus and Neptune or the Pioneer spacecraft. On this account the peturbations observed during the nineteenth century were due to a planet having a mass five times that of the Earth, whose orbit is tipped up relative to the orbits of the other planets and is also elongated. Thus Pioneer 10's failure to show any gravitational effect from this postulated planet can be explained because Planet 10 is too far away to do so. But between 1810 and 1910 it was near enough to affect both Uranus and Neptune. According to Anderson it is unlikely to affect the outer planets until the year 2000. (Littman, ibid, p.204)

It should be noted that the deviations in the motions of Uranus and Neptune are very slight, less than 1 arcsecond. In comparison the deviations in the orbit of Uranus, prior to the discovery of Neptune, were in the region of 100 arcseconds. Astronomers are divided over whether these deviations are the result of Planet 10 or the result of errors arising out of nineteenth-century data. It was only after 1910 that astronomers began to use micrometers to measure the positions of Uranus and Neptune. Calculations made before that date might well be unreliable.

At present there are very few clues regarding the whereabouts of Planet 10, although several investigations are underway. According to Harrington, Planet 10 is now heading away from the Earth and can be located in the southern sky, possibly in the constellation of Centaurus. (Croswell, 1990, p.35) He also claims that it once collided with Neptune thus causing the aberrations in the orbits of Neptune's moons, Triton and Nereid, and pushing Pluto - until then a satellite of Neptune - towards the Sun. Computer simulations, carried out by Harrington and Thomas van Flandern, concerning the characteristics a planet would require in order to produce these effects on Triton, Nereid and Pluto, suggest that it should have a mass and elongated orbit very similar to that attributed to Planet 10. Two other predictions for the location of Planet 10 have recently appeared. Conley Powell in Alabama predicts that it lies in the constellation of Virgo and is smaller than the Earth. In Brazil, Rodney Gomes and Sylvio Ferraz-Mello suggest that it may lie in the constellation of Cancer or Gemini. (Croswell, 1990, p.37)

It should, however, be stressed that observational errors in the estimated orbits of Neptune and Uranus should not be discounted. It is even possible that current knowledge of the law of gravity is incorrect, as it was before Einstein's General Theory of Relativity modified Newtonian theory. But few modern astronomers would assign a high level of probability to this hypothesis. Yet even if either alternatives were the case the search for a tenth planet need not be ruled out, although it would no longer be based on problems concerning alleged anomalies in the motions of the outer planets.

Figure IV

Problem	Explain aberrations in the orbits of Uranus and Neptune. The background theories require postulation of a mass of sufficient density to exert a gravitational effect on these planets.
	Initial Thinking
Solution 1	Predict additional planet in the Solar System.
	Preliminary Evaluation, Pursuit and Rule Out
Solution 1	Predict location and observe the planet, Pluto.
	Rule Out
	Pluto's mass is not adequate to fully explain the aberrations of the orbits of the outer planets.
	Pursuit
Solution 2	Pluto is either larger or denser than originally calculated.
Solution 3	There is a dim star orbiting the Sun, but further out than any of the planets.
Solution 4	There is a reservoir of comets just beyond the planets.
Solution 5	There is a tenth planet in the Solar

System.

Rule Out

Solution 2   Rule out after observations confirm
                                    Pluto's size and density.

Solutions 3,4.

                                    Rule out after checking data from
                                    space probes, which reveal no
                                    evidence to support existence of
                                    either a dim star or a group of
                                    comets of sufficient density.

Solution 5   This emerges as the most plausible
                                    and merits further pursuit.

Further Pursuit

Here new data is introduced with further tests for Solution 5.

                                    The initial problem is redefined

Problem Redefined

                                    What properties must Planet 10
                                    possess to be consistent with data
                                    which reveals that the peturbations
                                    only occurred between 1810 and
                                    1910?

Solution 1   Planet 10 must have a mass five
                                    times that of the Earth, and must
                                    pursue an elongated orbit around
                                    the Sun every 800 years.

Pursuit

Calculate the current position of Planet 10 and seek confirming observations.

Semmelweiss and the Problem of Cross Infection

Ignaz Semmelweiss was responsible for women patients in the Vienna Hospital during the mid-nineteenth century. The problem concerned women who were delivered of babies in the First Maternity Division as they were more likely than women in the Second Division to catch a fatal disease known as puerperal fever. Whereas the average death rate from puerperal fever was between 2% and 3% in Vienna, the death rate in the First Division was as high as 8.2%. Semmelweiss tackled this problem using Second Division cases as controls, which he compared with women in the First Division. (Trusted, 1979, pp.20-22)

Several solutions were proposed, evaluated, and ruled out, using a variety of methods some of which would violate contemporary ethical standards.

Among the initial proposals was the suggestion that there was an epidemic infection in the First Division. This was ruled out because such an epidemic would either die down or spread to the Second Division, which it did not. The idea that the death rate was due to overcrowding also had to be ruled out, as overcrowding was greater in the Second Division. Differences in diet were ruled out after both Divisions were given similar diets with no significant reduction in the moratility rates in the First Division.

There were suggestions that patients in the First Division were more roughly treated by the male medical students than patients in the Second Division who were treated by nuns. This was ruled out as an explanation of the mortality rate after it was pointed out that both male medical students and nuns received the same training. However, it was noted that the manner of delivery differed in each Division; in the Second Division patients were delivered on their sides. This suggestion was pursued but ruled out after no difference was observed following the adoption of a uniform method of delivery in both Divisions. A further suggestion introduced the possibility that psychological factors peculiar to the First Division might be worthy of pursuit. A priest taking the sacrament to a dying woman in the First Division had to pass through five wards before reaching the patient. This dramatic entrance of the priest, preceded by a man ringing a bell, it was suggested, might frighten the women. Patients in the Second Division were not alarmed in this way. However, this explanation was ruled out when no change was observed after the priest had been persuaded to dispense with the bell and procession through the wards.

The correct solution was eventually arrived at with the introduction of new data. One of Semmelweiss's colleagues contracted puerperal fever after he was punctured by a scalpel whilst conducting an autopsy. It was inferred that dead tissue from the corpse had caused the infection and sudden death. (This reasoning took place before theories of bacterial infection were adopted). Moreover, as students from the First Division performed dissections on corpses it seemed plausible to suggest that they could be carrying 'cadaveric matter' to their patients. If this were so then a regime of handwashing in chloride of lime (intended to destroy 'cadaveric matter') should reduce the mortality rate in the First Division. This suggestion was boosted by a fall in the death rate, after a regime of hand washing had been imposed, despite fierce resistance from physicians who resisted the implication that their hands could be 'carriers of death'. In 1848 the death rate in the First Division fell to 1.27% compared with 1.37% in the Second Division. Having thus established a link between 'cadaveric matter' and puerperal fever Semmelweiss then performed one further test. Semmelweiss and his colleagues examined a women who was dying of a festering cervical cancer. Then, without hand washing, they examined twelve other women who consequently died of puerperal fever. The experiment was successful and the hypothesis confirmed. The ethical objections are self-evident.

Now Semmelweiss did not blindly conjecture and falsify, nor were his hypotheses merely of psychological interest. They were based on long standing medical experience (heuristics) which regulated the generation of plausible solutions. A less experienced physician would not have been able to make use of the new data provided by his colleague's death. But Semmelweiss's heuristics were nevertheless crude, and amounted to a small improvement over a blanket trial and error search when compared with the heuristics available to physicians aware of theories of bacterial infection. A contemporary medical student, transported back into the mid-nineteenth century, would operate with a more efficient solution restrictor. But even possessed with the limited heuristics of the time there is a case for employing further pursuit to the suggestion that the death rate may have been influenced by the fact that it was male medical students (who also performed autopsies) rather than nuns, who treated patients in the First Division.

Figure V

Problem   Explain high Mortality rates in the
                                 First Maternity Division in the
                                 Vienna Hospital during the 1840's.

                                 Initial Thinking

163

Solution 1	Epidemic in the First Division.
Solution 2	Overcrowding is the cause of the death rate.
Solution 3	Inferior diet in the First Division.
Solution 4	Factors peculiar to therapy from male medical students.
Solution 5	Manner of delivery.
Solution 6	Psychological factors.
	Preliminary Evaluation, Pursuit and Rule Out.
Solution 1	Rule out because the disease neither spreads nor dies out.
Solution 2	Rule out because overcrowding is greater in the Second Division.
Solution 3	Rule out after observing effects of similar diets.
Solution 4	Rule out because both medical students and nuns receive similar training.
Solution 5	Rule out after observing effects of a uniform method of delivery.
Solution 6	Rule out after observing no improvement after removal of psychological factors.

At this point new data is introduced and the initial problem is enlarged.

Problem	Explain high mortality rates in the First Maternity Division and death of colleague whilst conducting an autopsy.
	Further Pursuit
Solution 7	'Cadaveric matter' carried from corpses to patients by medical students. Corroborated by fall in mortality

rate after hand washing.

Comment.

In this example solution 7 is worthy of adoption, though by no means wholly accurate as an adequate explanation would have to address the issue of bacterial causes of disease. It should also be noted that solution 4 might have yielded positive results were it subjected to further pursuit. Medical students, in this case, were transmittors of the disease and further pursuit may have ruled out rough treatment whilst leaving open the possibility of further investigation of the therapy provided by male medical students. In the foregoing examples it was clear that reasons were given for ruling out some suggestions whilst entertaining and pursuing others. Moreover, given a clear grasp of the problems there was nothing mysterious or irrational in the process of generating, regulating and explaining any of the proposed solutions. Yet according to the two-context theory all of this would have to be exempt from rational assessment, as a complete and finished piece of research had not been presented for evaluation. But in the foregoing examples it can be seen that modes of reasoning, which allegedly belong only in the context of justification, are employed throughout the entire process of discovery. In actual practice, scientists and creative problem solvers employ various strategies as they go along, thinking up, comparing, sorting and rejecting solutions. Preliminary evaluation, with its pursuit and rule out phases, is an essential characteristic of discovery. It is essential also to the notion of discovery as a process. For as a process a discovery may take an indeterminate length of time which cannot be assimilated to an act of judgement, as the two-context theory requires.

Adoption

The final stage, adoption, need not be incompatible with traditional criteria for the assessment of completed theories or research reports, although an adopted theory need not be accepted in any absolute sense and may accordingly be returned to the stage of preliminary evaluation. Refuted theories can and do return to 'defeat the defeaters'. Feyerabend (1987, p.263) draws attention to the fact that atomic theory was regarded as a metaphysical monster in the nineteenth century, in conflict with known facts and internally incoherent. Rule out is never absolute. Facts and theories can be reconstructed (Nickles, 1988) in the light of new interests, and background theories which form the basis of rule out, can be displaced, thus allowing that which was ruled out to re-emerge as a plausible line of research. But a rejection of rule out as an absolute irreversible aspect of scientific development is perfectly compatible with the recognition that rule out is indispensible to scientific research, just as a recognition that some initial thoughts are plausible is compatible with the fact that some are not. It is simply that criteria for rule out cannot, and should not, guarantee correct judgements on every occasion. It is sufficient to recognise that some ideas just have to be ruled out in order to pursue more plausible or entertaining options.

When characterising the final stages in the process of discovery there are several pitfalls to avoid. It is most important to avoid expressions which reinforce images of excessive objectivity and ultimate certainty. The term 'adoption' has been chosen here to reflect the more dynamic and changing aspects of scientific development. For various reasons theories and explanations are adopted by scientists and laypersons. The term 'adoption' avoids commitment to certainty with its muddle of psychology, theories of knowledge, opinion, probability, along with belief and assent. The term 'acceptance' does not carry the dynamic overtones of science as a process. It is as if everything stops when something is finally accepted. Adoption indicates an air of satisfaction, but it is also suggestive of the practical aspects of putting a theory to work, making it fit, and incorporating it into work in progress. Although it suggests satisfaction, 'adoption' does not imply confidence. An adopted theory may still be on trial, pending stronger evaluation, further pursuit, and possible rule out. It may have been adopted because it was the best choice among unappealing alternatives. But most important, it suggests flexibility, allowing opportunity for further work, more fitting, more connections, and more reconstruction.

Adoption is not incompatible with revision and updating. By its very nature science is a self correcting enterprise. Immunity from correction and rule out is not a measure of success; in some instances it merely indicates dogma and sterility. It is also possible that the same reasons would be cited for the adoption of a theory as for preliminary evaluation. It may be that there are more grounds, more reasons, more evidence, greater aesthetic appeal, for adoption, or that most of the leading alternatives have been decisively ruled out. In all of these cases reasons can be cited, examined, and their pros and cons evaluated.

Adoption may be instant, as in cases involving 'effective surprise' where an unconventional solution is accepted immediately, (Bruner, 1965, p.3) or it may take time, as in the case of Copernican theory. If one demands strict criteria for adoption then Galileo's elements of mechanics could not have been fully adopted before Newton. But they were part of canonical knowledge before then. And even Newton 'needed divine intervention to keep the planetary system in order'. (Feyerabend, 1987, p.258)

Broadly speaking, a theory or hypothesis is adopted when it has emerged through the various stages in the process of discovery outlined above. In some cases a theory may be deemed adoptible whilst still remaining in the rule out phase; that is, held until it is replaced by a better one. As such adoption would conform to Popper's ideas, according to which scientific statements or conjectures are held until future possible falsification. One important difference between the position outlined here and Popper's overall view is that it is not maintained here that the possible instability of an adoptable theory has any bearing on attempts to demarcate between scientific statements and pseudo scientific statements. Another difference is that whereas the standard H-D approach concentrates upon the testing of already completed theories, the foregoing account allows for the possibility of tests which are relevant in all stages of hypothesis formation.

There is a sense in which adoption is a redundant category. Having completed a rule out phase a theory can be adopted without further tests. Nevertheless, an adopted theory will usually have met some of the following conditions.

1. Receive an increasing number of confirming instances which should be varied. That is, an adopted theory would require more than one type of supporting instances; Newton's theory of universal gravitation was not supported merely by numerous instances of falling apples, but with confirmed predictions from both terrestrial and celestial sources.

2. Exhibit a degree of compatibility with well established theories and facts. Einstein's General Theory of Relativity did not merely rule out rivals, part of its appeal lay in its consistency throughout the entire realm of physics.

3. Where there is incompatibility the new theory should possess superior explanatory power and the ability to explain the incompatibility, and also indicate what was wrong with established theories and data. If, for example, Einstein's General Theory of Relativity had only explained the results of the Michelson-Morley experiment and nothing else, it would not have been adopted so readily.

4.   Rule out the main competitors as the theory is pursued. For example, as the Copernican theory was pursued, much of the Aristotelian edifice was dismantled by it.

5.   Following the stage of solution generation a new theory should receive confirmation which was not necessarily anticipated during the initial stage. For example, the confirming instance of the discovery of Neptune for Newtonian theory. In this respect new theories may derive additional support from serendipitous events. 'Maxwell's electromagnetic theory unexpectedly explained the phenomenon of light, and in addition predicted the existence of radio waves, establishing relations between optical and electromagnetic phenomena'. (Kantorovich and Ne'eman, 1989, p.516)

It should be stressed that whilst many of the above-mentioned criteria for adoption may be present in numerous successful theories, they are not universal guidelines for theory adoption. Increased explanatory content, adequacy of factual data, confirmation, survival of rule out, might all be set aside. Feyerabend (1987, p.255) considers the possibility that a modern Galileo might still have to appeal to extra-scientific criteria for the adoption of his theories.

Our modern Galileo will also find that the arguments only rarely suffice to get an idea accepted and financed. The idea must fit the ideology of the institute that is supposed to absorb it and must agree with the ways in which research is done there.

Even within the scientific community criteria for adoption varies widely.

What would have been the judgement of modern scientists and philosophers of science had they been transferred into the early seventeenth century and asked the question Bellarmo was asked, namely: What's your opinion of Copernicus? The answer is that different people would have said different things. Science, like any other enterprise, knows hardliners and it knows tolerant people. There are scientists who are satisfied with simplicity and intellectual

168

experiment and there are other scientists who regard such inconsistencies as natural companions of progress. Michelson and Rutherford never fully accepted relativity, Poincare, Lorentz and Ehrenfest became doubtful after Kaufmann's experiments, while Planck and Einstein, convinced by its internal symmetry, were more persistent. Sommerfield was never successful in making the older quantum theory as formidable as classical celestial mechanics while Bohr, despite the successes achieved, thought Sommerfield was on the wrong track. Pauling loved confusing his colleagues with conjectures taken from simple-model building while they preferred pondering the intricacies of X-ray photographs. (Feyerabend, 1987, pp.256-7)

It might be objected that what Feyerabend cites as criteria for adoption does not significantly differ from criteria for preliminary evaluation. Feyerabend would probably endorse this view insisting that there is no essential difference between the respective contexts of discovery and justification. But the rejection of the two-context theory need not involve any commitment to the view that discovery is an irrational affair. Criteria for preliminary evaluation, pursuit, rule out and adoption does vary among scientists. But this does not invalidate the above account of discovery as a process involving various stages, each of which is amenable to rational assessment. Scientists may have good reasons for recognising problems, good reasons for generating solutions, entertaining them, rejecting or adopting them.

Bibliography

Achinstein, Peter. (1971), Law and Explanation, Oxford University Press, London.

_____ (1980), 'Discovery and Rule Books', in Thomas Nickles (ed), Scientific Discovery, Logic, and Rationality, D. Reidel, Dordrecht, pp.117-137.

Anderson, Douglas R. (1987), Creativity and the Philosophy of C.S. Peirce, Nijhoff, Dordrecht.

Black, Max. (1962), Models and Metaphors, Columbia University-Press, New York.

Boden, Margaret, (1977) Artificial Intelligence, Harvester, Brighton.

Bohm, David and Peat, David. (1988), Science, Order and Creativity, Routledge, London.

Bondi, Hermann. (1981), 'What is Progress in Science?' in Stuart Brown, John Fauvel and Ruth Finnegan (eds), Conceptions of Inquiry, Methuen, London, pp.123-27)

Boyle, Robert. (1772), The Works of the Honourable Robert Boyle, (ed), T.Birch, London.

Born, Max.(1923), 'Quantentheorie und Storungsrechnung', Die Naturwissenschaften, 27, pp.537-50.

Braithwaite, R. (1953), Scientific Explanation, Cambridge University Press, Cambridge.

Brannigan, Augustine, (1981), The Social Basis of Scientific Discovery, Cambridge University Press, Cambridge.

Briskman, L. (1981), 'Creative Product and Creative Process in Science and Art', in D. Dutton and M. Krausz (eds), The Concept of Creativity in Science and Art, Nijhoff, The Hague, pp.129-56.

Bruner, Jerome S. (1967), 'The Conditions of Creativity', in Howard E. Gruber, Glenn Terrell, Michael Wertheimer (eds), Contemporary Approaches to Creative Thinking, Atherton, New York, pp.1-30.

Buchanan, B.G. (1969), 'Heuristic Dendral: A Program for Generating Explanatory Hypothesis in Organic Chemistry', Machine Intelligence, 4, American Elsevier, New York.

_____(1985), 'Steps Towards Mechanizing Discovery?', in Kenneth F. Schaffner (ed), Logic of Discovery and Diagnosis in Medicine, University of California Press, Berkeley, pp.94-114.

Burian, Richard, M. (1987), 'How Not to Talk About Conceptual Change in Science', in Joseph C. Pitt and Marcello Pera (eds), Rational Change in Science, D. Reidel, Dordrecht, pp.1-33.

Chandrasekhar, S. (1987), Truth and Beauty, University of Chicag Press, Chicago.

Clignet, Remi. (1985), The Structure of Artistic Revolutions, Philadelphia University Press, Philadelphia.

Cohen, I.B. (1983), The Newtonian Revolution, Cambridge University Press, Cambridge.

Conan Doyle, Sir Arthur. (1981), The Penguin Complete Sherlock Holmes, Penguin, Middlesex.

Croswell, Ken (1990), 'The Hunt for Planet X', New Scientist, December, 22., pp.34-37.

Crowe, Michael J. (1988), The Extraterrestrial Life Debate: 1750-1900: The Idea of a Plurality of Worlds From Kant to Lowell, Cambridge University Press, Cambridge.

Curd, Martin V. (1980), 'Logic of Discovery: Three Approaches', in Thomas Nickles (ed), Scientific Discovery, Logic and Rationality, D.Reidel, Dordrecht, pp.201-19.

Darwin, Charles. (1925), The Life and Letters of Charles Darwin, Appleton, New York.

Davies, P.C.W. and Brown, J. (1988), Superstrings: A Theory of Everything, Cambridge University Press, Cambridge.

Descartes, Rene. (1911), Descartes Philosophical Writing, translated by E.S. Haldane and G.R.T. Ross, Cambridge University Press, Cambridge.

Dreyfus, Hubert L. (1972), What Computers Can't Do, Harper and Row, New York.

Einstein, Albert. (1939), The World As I See It, translated by Alan Harris, Bodley Head, London.

Erwin, Edward. (1988), 'Testing Freudian Hypotheses', in D. Batens and J.P. van Benegem (eds), Theory and Experiment, D. Reidel, Dordrecht.

Estling, Ralph. (1990), 'Leg Before Cricket', New Scientist, 24.November, p.67.

Feyerabend, Paul K. (1961), 'Comments on Hanson's "Is There a Logic of Scientific Discovery?"', in Herbert Feigl and Grover Maxwell (eds), Current Issues in the Philosophy of Science, Holt, Rinehart and Winston.

_____ (1975), Against Method, New Left Books, London.

_____ (1987), Farewell to Reason, Verso, London.

Feynman, Richard. (1967), The Character of Physical Law, M.I.T. Press, Cambridge, Mass.

French, Roger. (1989) 'Harvey in Holland: Circulation and the Calvinists', in R. French and A. Wear (eds), The Medical Revolution of the Seventeenth Century, Cambridge University Press, Cambridge, pp.46-86.

Gick, M.L. and Holyoak, K.J. (1980), 'Analogical Problem Solving', Cognitive Psychology, 12, pp.306-55.

Giere, Ronald, N. (1988), Explaining Science: A Cognitive Approach, University of Chicago Press, London.

Glymour, Clark. (1980), Theory and Evidence, Princeton University Press.

Goodman, Nelson and Elgin, Catherine Z. (1988), Reconceptions in Philosophy and Other Arts and Sciences, Routledge, London.

Grigson, Caroline. (1990), 'Missing Links in the Piltdown Fraud', New Scientist, 13. January, pp.55-8.

Gross, Alan G. (1990), The Rhetoric of Science, Harvard Univers Press, Cambridge, Mass.

Grunbaum, Adolf. (1979), 'Is Freudian Psychoanalytic Theory Pseudo-Scientific by Karl Popper's Criterion of Demarcation?', American Philosophical Quarterly, 16, 2. pp.131-41.

Gunderson, Keith. (1985), Mentality and Machines, Croom Helm, London.

Gutting, Gary. (1980), 'The Logic of Invention', in Thomas Nickles (ed), Scientific Discovery, Logic and Rationality, D. Reidel, Dordrecht, pp.221-34.

Habermas, Jurgen. (1972), Knowledge and Human Interests, translated by J. Shapiro, Heinemann, London.

Hadamard, Jacques. (1945), The Psychiatry of Invention in the Mathematical Field, Princeton University Press, Princeton.

Hanson, Norwood R. (1958a), Patterns of Discovery, Cambridge University Press, Cambridge.

_____(1958b), 'The Logic of Discovery', The Journal of Philosophy, LV, 25, pp.1073-89.

_____(1961), 'Is There a Logic of Scientific Discovery?', in Herbert Feigl and Grover Maxwell (eds), Current Issues in the Philosophy of Science, Holt, Rinehart and Winston, pp.20-42.

_____(1961-2), 'Retroductive Inference', in Bernard Baumrin (ed), Philosophy of Science, The Delaware Seminar, Vol. I, John Wiley, New York, pp.21-37.

_____(1963), The Concept of the Positron, Cambridge University Press, Cambridge.

_____(1965), 'Notes Towards a Logic of Discovery', in Richard J. Bernstein (ed), Critical Essays on Charles Sanders Peirce, Greenwood Press, Connecticut, pp.42-65.

_____(1967), 'An Anatomy of Discovery', The Journal of Philosophy, LXIV, 11, pp.321-52.

_____(1971), 'The Zenith and Nadir of Classical Mechanics', in What I Do Not Believe and Other Essays, S. Toulmin and H. Woolf (eds), D. Reidel, Dordrecht, pp.359-78.

Harre, Rom. (1981), 'Creativity in Science', in D. Dutton and M. Krausz, Creativity in Science and Art, Martinus Nijhoff, The Hague, pp.19-46.

Hattiangadi, J.N. (1980), 'The Vanishing Context of Discovery', in Thomas Nickles (ed), Scientific Discovery, Logic and Rationality, D. Reidel, Dordrecht, pp.257-65.

Haugeland, John. (1987), 'Semantic Engines: An Introduction to Mind Design', in John Haugeland (ed), Mind Design, M.I.T. Press, Cambridge, Mass, pp.1-34.

Hausman, C.A. (1981), 'Criteria of Creativity', in D. Dutton and M. Krausz (eds), Creativity in Science and Art, Martinus Nijhoff, The Hague, pp. 75-90.

Hegel, G.W.F. (1975), Jena Lectures, cited by G. Lukacs in The Young Hegel, trans. R. Livingstone, Merlin, London.

Heisenberg, Werner. (1971), Physics and Beyond, Harper and Row, New York.

Hempel, Carl G. (1966), Philosophy of Natural Science, Engelwood Cliffs, New Jersey.

_____(1985), 'Thoughts on Limitations of Discovery', in Kenneth F. Schaffner (ed), Logic of Discovery and Diagnosis in Medicine, University of California Press, Berkeley, pp.115- 22.

Henbest, Nigel. (1987), 'Ageing Space Probes Signal the Presence of a New Planet', New Scientist, 16.July, p.36.

Hesse, Mary B. (1970), Models and Analogies in Science, University of Notre Dame Press, Notre Dame.

Holland, John H., Holyoak., Keith, J, Nisbett., Richard, E., Thogard, Paul, R. (1986), Induction: Processes of Inference, Learning and Discovery, M.I.T. Press, Cambridge, Mass.

Hull, David L. (1988), Science as a Process, University of Chicago Press, Chicago.

Jackson, K.F. (1975), The Art of Solving Problems, Heinemann, London.

Jarvie, I.C. (1981), 'The Rationality of Creativity', in D. Dutton and M. Krausz (eds), The Concept of Creativity in Science and Art, Martinus Nijhoff, The Hague, pp.109-28.

Kantorovitch, Aharon and Ne'eman, Yuval. (1989), 'Serendipity as a Source of Evolutionary Progress in Science', Studies in the History of Philosophy of Science, 20, 4, pp.505-29.

Kivenson, Gilbert. (1977), The Art of Science and Invention, Van Nostrand Reinhold Company, New York.

Kneller, George, F. (1978), Science as a Human Endeavour, Columbia University Press, New York.

Koestler, Arthur. (1975), The Act of Creation, Pan, London.

_____(1981), 'The Three Domains of Creativity', in D. Dutton and M. Krausz (eds), The Concept of Creativity in Science and Art, Martinus Nijhoff, The Hague, pp.1-18.

Kordig, Carl R. (1978), 'Discovery and Justification', Philosophy of Science, 45, pp.110-17.

Kuhn, Thomas S. (1957), The Copernican Revolution, Chicago University Press, Chicago.

_____(1970a), 'Logic of Discovery or Psychology of Research' in I. Lakatos and A. Musgrave (eds), Criticism and the Growth of Knowledge, Cambridge University Press, Cambridge, pp.1-23.

_____(1970), The Structure of Scientific Revolutions, Chicago University Press, Chicago.

_____ (1977), The Essential Tension, Chicago University Press, Chicago.

Lakatos, Imre. (1970), 'Falsification and the Methodology of Scientific Research Programmes', in I. Lakatos and A. Musgrave (eds), Criticism and the Growth of Knowledge, Cambridge University Press, Cambridge, pp.91-196.

Lamb, David and Easton, Susan M. (1984), Multiple Discovery, Avebury, Aldershot.

Langley, Pat. (1979), 'Rediscovering Physics with BACON 3', Proceedings of the Sixth International Joint Conference on Artificial Intelligence, pp.505-7.

Langley, Pat., Simon, Herbert A., Bradshaw, Gary L., and Zytkow, Jan M. (1987), Scientific Discovery: Computational Exploration of the Creative Process, M.I.T. Press, Cambridge, Mass.

Lashchyk, Eugene. (1986), 'Heuristics for Scientific and Literary Creativity: The Role of Models, Analogies and Metaphors', in J.Margolis, M. Krauzs and R.M. Burian (eds), Rationality, Relativism and the Human Sciences, Martinus Nijhoff, The Hague, pp.151-185.

Laudan, Larry. (1980), 'Why Abandon Logic of Discovery?', in Thomas Nickles (ed), Scientific Discovery, Logic, and Rationality, D. Reidel, Dordrecht, pp.173-83.

Laudan, Rachael. (1987), 'The Rationality of Entertainment and Pursuit', in Joseph C. Pitt and Marcello Pera (eds), Rational Changes in Science, D. Reidel, Dordrecht, pp.203-20.

Leatherdale, W.H. (1974), The Role of Analogy Model and Metaphor in Science, North Holland Publishing Co., Amsterdam.

Lenat, D.B. (1977), 'Automated Theory Formation in Mathematics', Proceedings of the Fifth International Joint Conference on Artificial Intelligence.

_____ (1983), 'EURISCO: A Program that Learns New Heuristics and Domain Concepts', Artificial Intelligence, 21, pp,61-98.

Littman, Mark. (1989), Planets Beyond: Discovering the Outer Solar System, Wiley, New York.

Longino, Helen E. (1989), Science As Social Knowledge, Princeton University Press, New Jersey.

Lugg, Andrew. (1989), 'History, Discovery and Induction: Whewellon Kepler on the Orbit of Mars', in James Robert Brown and Jurgen Mittelstrasse (eds), An Intimate Relation, Studies in the History and Philosophy of Science, Kluwer, Boston/Dordrecht, pp.283-98.

Luria, S.E. (1985), A Slot Machine, A Broken Test Tube, New York.

Matthews, Harrison. (1981), 'The Case of the Pleistocene Cricket Bat', New Scientist, June 25.

McMullin, Ernan. (1985), 'Diagnosing By Computer', in Kenneth F. Schaffner (ed), Logic of Discovery and Diagnosis in Medicine, University of California Press, Berkeley, pp.199-222.

Millar, P. (1972), The Piltdown Man, Gollancz, London.

Miller, Arthur I. (1986), Imagery in Scientific Thought: Creating 20th. Century Physics, M.I.T. Press, Boston.

Morison, Elting E. (1966), Men, Machines, and Modern Times, M.I.T. Press, Cambridge, Mass.

Munevar, Gonzalo. (1989), 'Science as Part of Nature', in Kai Hahlweg and C.A. Hooker (eds), Issues in Evolutionary Epistemology, State University of New York Press, Albany, pp.475-87.

Myers, Jack D. (1985), 'The Process of Clinical Diagnosis and its Adaption to the Computer', in Kenneth F. Schaffner (ed), Logic of Discovery and Diagnosis in Medicine, University of California Press, Berkeley, pp.155-80.

Newell, Allen, Shaw, J.C. and Simon, H.A. (1967), 'The Process of Creative Thinking', in Howard E. Grubner, Glenn Terrell, Michael Wertheimer (eds), Contemporary Approaches to Creative Thinking, Atherton, New York, pp.63-119.

Nickles, Thomas. (1987), 'Methodology and Heuristics', in Joseph C. Pitt and Marcello Pera (eds), Rational Change in Science, D.Reidel, Dordrecht, pp.103-32.

_____(1988), 'Reconstructing Science: Discovery and Experiment', in D.Batens and J.P. van Benegem (eds), Theory and Experiment, D.Reidel, Dordrecht, pp.33-53.

_____(1989), 'Heuristic Appraisal: A Proposal', Social Epistemology, 3. 3. pp.175-88.

Passmore, John. (1968), A Hundred Years of Philosophy, Penguin, Middlesex.

Pauling, Linus. (1977), 'A Chat With Linus Pauling', G. Leeson, California Living, (section of the San Francisco Sunday Examiner and Chronicle), July,17th.

Peirce, Charles Sanders. (1931-58), Collected Papers of Charles Sanders Peirce, Charles Hartshorne, Paul Weiss and Arthur Burks (eds), 8.volumes, Harvard University Press, Cambridge, Mass.

_____(1957), Essays in the Philosophy of Science, V.Thomas (ed), Bobbs Merrill, New York.

_____(1968), 'A Neglected Argument for the Reality of God', in B. Brady and N. Capaldi (eds), Science: Men, Methods, Goals, New York, pp.143-9.

_____(1983), 'A Theory of Probable Inference', in C.S. Peirce (ed), Studies in Logic, John Betjamins, Amsterdam, pp.143-9.

Planck, Max. (1949), Autobiography, American Philosophical Library, New York.

Poincare, Henri J. (1952), 'Mathematical Genius', in Brewster Ghiselin (ed), The Creative Process, New York.

Polanyi, Michael. (1958), Personal Knowledge, Routledge, London.

_____(1966), Knowing and Being, Routledge, London.

_____(1981), 'The Creative Imagination', in D.Dutton and M.Krausz (eds), The Concept of Creativity in Science and Art, Martinus Nijhoff, The Hague, pp.91-108.

Polya, G. (1957), How To Solve It, Princeton University Press, Princeton.

Pople, Harry E. Jr. (1985), 'Coming to Grips With the Multiple Diagnosis Problem', in Kenneth F. Schaffner (ed), Logic of Discovery and Diagnosis in Medicine, University of California Press, Berkeley, pp.181-98.

Popper, Sir Karl R. (1959), The Logic of Scientific Discovery, Hutchinson, London.

_____(1963), Conjectures and Refutations, Routledge, London.

_____(1972), Objective Knowledge: An Evolutionary Approach, Clarendon Press, Oxford.

Reichenbach, Hans. (1958), The Rise of Scientific Philosophy, University of California Press, Berkeley.

Rescher, Nicholas. (1978), Peirce's Philosophy of Science, Notre Dame University Press, Notre Dame.

Rohrlich, Fritz. (1987), From Paradox to Reality, Cambridge University Press, Cambridge.

Russell, Bertrand. (1937), The Scientific Outlook, Unwin, London.

Salmon, Wesley C. (1970), 'Bayes's Theorem and the History of Science', in Roger H. Stuewer (ed), Minnesota Studies in the Philosophy of Science, Volume 5, University of Minnesota Press, Minneapolis, pp.68-86.

Schaffner, Kenneth F. (1980), 'Discovery in the Biomedial Sciences: Logic or Irrational Intuition?', in Kenneth F. Schaffner (ed), Scientific Discovery: Case Studies, D.Reidel, Dordrecht, pp.171-205.

_____(1985) ed. Logic of Discovery and Diagnosis in Medicine, University of California Press, Berkeley.

Scheines, Richard. (1987), 'Automating Creativity', in James H. Fetzer (ed), Aspects of Artificial Intelligence, Kluwer, Dordrecht, pp.339-65.

Schon, Donald. (1969), Invention and the Evolution of Ideas, Tavistock, London.

Shea, William R. (1987), 'The Quest for Scientific Rationality: Some Historical Considerations', in Joseph C. Pitt and Marcello Pera (eds), Rational Change in Science, D.Reidel, Dordrecht, pp.155-76.

Simon, Herbert A. (1977), Models of Discovery, D.Reidel, Dordrecht.

_____(1985), 'Artificial Intelligence Approaches to Problem Solving and Clinical Diagnosis', in Kenneth F. Schaffner (ed), Logic of Discovery and Diagnosis in Medicine, University of California Press, Berkeley, pp.72-93.

Simon, Herbert A., Langley, P. and Bradshaw, G.L. (1981), 'Scientific Discovery as Problem Solving', Synthese, 47, pp.1- 27.

Slansky, Richard C. (1988), 'Towards a Unified Theory', in Necia Grant Cooper and Geoffrey B. West (eds), Particle Physics: A Los Alamos Primer, Cambridge University Press, Cambridge, pp.72-85.

Sparshott, F.E. (1981), 'Every Horse has a Mouth: A Personal Poetics', in D. Dutton and M. Krausz (eds), The Concept of Creativity in Science and Art, Martinus Nijhoff, The Hague, pp.47-74.

Spencer, Frank. (1990), Piltdown: A Scientific Forgery, Oxford University Press, Oxford.

Spender, Stephen. (1970), 'The Making of a Poem, in P.E.Vernon (ed), Creativity, Penguin, Middlesex, pp.61-76.

Stent, G.S. (1972), 'Prematurity and Uniqueness in Scientific Discovery', Scientific American, 227, pp.84-93.

Stringer, Chris. (1990), 'The Piltdown Conman', The Guardian, 22. June, p.28.

Trusted, Jennifer. (1979), The Logic of Scientific Inference, Macmillan, London.

Wartofsky, Marx. (1980), 'Judgement, Creativity and Discovery', in Thomas Nickles (ed), Scientific Discovery: Case Studies, D.Reidel, Dordrecht, pp.1-16.

Watanabe, Satosi. (1985), Pattern Recognition: Human and Mechanical, Wiley, New York

Weizenbaum, Joseph. (1984), Computer Power and Human Reason, Penguin, Middlesex.

West, Geoffrey B. (1988), 'Scale and Dimension - From Animals to Quarks', in Necia Grant Cooper and Geoffrey B. West (eds), Particle Physics: A Los Alamos Primer, Cambridge University Press, Cambridge, pp.1-21.

Whewell, William. (1968), 'Mr Mills' Logic', in William Whewell's Theory of Scientific Method, University of Pittsburgh Press, Pittsburgh.

_____(1847), Philosophy of the Inductive Sciences, Founded Upon Their History, second edition, Volume II, London.

Wilber, Ken. (1983), (ed), The Holographic Paradox and Other Paradoxes, Shambala, London.

Zahar, Elie. (1983), 'Logic of Discovery or Psychology of Invention?', British Journal of Philosophy of Science, 34, pp.243-61.

Zuckerman, Lord Solly. (1990) 'A New Clue to the Real Piltdown Forger', New Scientist, November 3, p.16.

Index

Crowe, M. 95
Curd, M. 50,139-40
cyclotron 99,119

Darwin, C. 9,17,19-20,24,53,
   133,145
Davy, H. 85
Dawson, C. 17-22
deduction 36,41,64,102
DEEP THOUGHT, 97,100
demons 55
DENDRAL, 108,111,115
Descartes, R. 2,25,60,100,104,
   107,117
diagnosis 135-139
Dreyfus, H.L. 89

Ehrlich, P. 86
Einstein, A.
7,38-39,72,83-85,87,97,99,100,
   133-4,146-7,167
Elgin, C.Z. 104
Eliot, T.S. 12

Elliot Smith, G. 19
Ellison, R. 8
Erwin, E. 149
Estling, R. 22

falsification 3,38,46-46,148-9
Fermi, E. 35-36
Feyerabend, P.K. 2,11,37,40,
   44-47,165-9
Feynman, R. 25,29-30
Fisher, B. 57
French, R. 10
Freud, S. 141,148-9

Galileo, G. 44,46-47,56,62,79,83,
   107,118,141,166,168
GENERAL PROBLEM
   SOLVER, 88-90

Giere, R.N. 99,103,135
GLAUBER, 93
Goodman, N. 104
Gordon, W.J.J. 59
Grigson, C. 20-21
Gross, A.G 113
Grunbaum, A. 148
Gutting, G. 97

Habermas, J. 61-62
Hamlet, 42,95,119-120
Hadamard, J. 86
Hanson, N.J. 3,26,40,61,66-80,
   121,155
Harrington, R.S. 158
Harvey, W. 10,131
Hattiangadi, J.N. 31
Haugeland, J. 95-96
Hegel, G.W.F. 13,100
Hempel, C.G. 28-29,112-3
Herschell, W. 150-1
Hesse, M. 132
heuristics 56-56,58,59,86,102-116
Hinton, M. 22
Holland, J.H. 114,123-6
Holmes, S. 110-111
Hull, D.L. 34
Hume,D. 2,25,104,130

induction 2,41,71,122
Interferon, 105
INTERNIST, 113,137-8

Jackson, J.F. 58
James, H. 55
Jarvie, I. 15

Kant,I. 38,55
Kantorovich, A. 81,116,168
Keith, A. 20-22
Kekule, F.A. 52-54,56

Kepler, J. 24,26,69-71,74-75,91
103,107,114-5,147
Kneller, G.F. 36
Koestler, A. 2,28,37,40,48-55,59
122-3
Kuhn, T. 11,24,31-33,50-51,113
116,129,150

Lakatos, I. 44-45
Langham, I. 21
Langley, P. 81-86,120
Laschyk, E. 51,126
Laudan, L. 77,142-3
Laudan, R. 143-4
Lenat, D.B. 91-93
Lighthill, J. 96
Littman, M. 151-2
Locke,J. 25
LOGIC THEORIST, 90-91
Longino, H. 105
Lowell, P. 157
Lugg, A. 26
Luria, S.E. 46

Mars 69-70,72,103
Marx, K. 131,134,149-50
Maskelyne, N. 151
Matthews, H. 22
McMullin, E. 137
Melville, H. 57
Mendel, G. 24-25
Merton, R. 11
metaphor 126-130
Michaelangelo, 25
Mill, J.S. 61
Millar, R. 19
Miller, A.I. 115
models, 133-35
de Morgan, A. 26
Morrison, E.E. 119-20
Mozart, W.A. 57
Munevar, G. 10,25

MYCIN, 113
Myers, J.D. 136-7

nature 9
Ne'eman, Y. 81,116,168
Neptune 72,152-4
Newell, A. 81,87-91,93-94,100-102,
109,120,139
Newton, I. 7,8,25,31,55,83,97,
103,107-8,152,166
Nickles, T. 23,28,104-5,165

Oakley, K. 18-19,21
observation 42,71,72,76,78
O'Hear, A. 128
Osborn, A. 59

Pauling, L. 111
Peat, D. 62,129
Peirce, C.S. 3,26,40,60-66,68,74,
79,86,94,97,102,104,106-7,130
Pickering, W.H. 157
Piltdown man 17-23,85
Planck, M. 10,84-85
Planet Ten 157-161
Plato, 7-9,56
plausibility 64-66,69
Pluto 157
poetry 11,13-15
Poincare, J.H. 37,52-54,115
Polya, G. 102
Polyani, M. 2,32,40-44,49,144
Pople, H. 136-7
Popper,K.2,15,28-29,32,37-48,51,
60 -67,71,74, 80,111,118-9,136,
142,148,167
positivism 8,61
Pound, E. 12
Powell, C. 159
Pribram, K. 131
Ptolemy, 7
puzzlement 42,62

quantum theory 86

reconstitution 17,23-25
Reichenbach, H. 2,28,37,66,71,
   74,80
relativity theory 87,146-7,159
retroduction 60,66,68,74-78
Russell, B. 41-43,91,93
Rutherford, E. 134

Salmon, W.C. 97-98,144-5
Sapp, J. 24
Sartre, J.P.14
scaling 98-99
Scheines, R. 99
Schaffner, K. 40,60,121-3,135-8,
   140
Schiller, F.C.S. 25
Schon, D. 8,126
Semmelweiss, I. 162-5
serendipity 116-7
Shakespeare, W. 59,95
Shaw, G.B. 55
Shaw, J.C. 88-89
Shea, W.R. 117-8
Simon, H.A. 8,40,57,61,81-84,
   88-89,95,100,103, 115,118,
   120,122,139
skepticism 2
Smith-Woodward, A. 17-18

Sollas,W.J. 19-20
Sparshott, F.E. 12-15
Spencer, F. 21
Spender, S. 14-15
Stringer, C. 22
surprise 56,65,78

tacit knowledge 42
Tombaugh, C. 157
Trusted, J. 162

unconventionality 55-58
Uranus 150-2

Venus 98,133
Vulcan 154-6

Wartofski, M. 32
Watanabe, S. 89
Wegener, A. 134-5
West, G.B. 99
Weizenbaum, J. 89
Whewell, W. 26,60
Whitehead, A.N. 91,93
Wilber, K. 131
Wittgenstein, L. 1
WISARD 89-90,96

Zahar, E. 84
Zuckerman, S. 22